AS Music
Revision Guide

AQA

Richard Knight

R. RHINEGOLD
EDUCATION

www.rhinegoldeducation.co.uk

Music Study Guides
GCSE, AS and A2 Music Study Guides (AQA, Edexcel and OCR)
GCSE, AS and A2 Music Listening Tests (AQA, Edexcel and OCR)
AS/A2 Music Technology Study Guide, Listening Tests and Revision Guide (Edexcel)
Revision Guides for GCSE (AQA, Edexcel and OCR), AS and A2 Music (Edexcel and OCR)

Also available from Rhinegold Education
Key Stage 3 Listening Tests: Book 1 and Book 2
AS and A2 Music Harmony Workbooks
GCSE and AS Music Composition Workbooks
GCSE and AS Music Literacy Workbooks
Romanticism in Focus, Baroque Music in Focus, Modernism in Focus, *The Immaculate Collection* in Focus,
Who's Next in Focus, *Batman* in Focus, *Goldfinger* in Focus, Musicals in Focus
Music Technology from Scratch
Understanding Popular Music

First published 2012 in Great Britain by
Rhinegold Education
14–15 Berners Street
London W1T 3LJ

www.rhinegoldeducation.co.uk

© Rhinegold Education 2012
a division of Music Sales Limited

You should always check the current requirements of the examination, as these may change. Copies of the AQA specification can be downloaded from the AQA website at www.aqa.org.uk or may be purchased from AQA publications, Unit Two, Wheel Forge Way, Trafford Park, Manchester, M17 1EH. Telephone: 0844 209 6614   Fax: 0161 953 1177   Email: publications@aqa.org.uk

AQA AS Music Revision Guide
Order No. RHG106
ISBN: 978-1-78038-242-5

Exclusive Distributors:
Music Sales Ltd
Distribution Centre, Newmarket Road
Bury St Edmunds, Suffolk IP33 3YB, UK

Printed in the EU

Companion website: www.hybridpublications.com
Access code: EK193

Contents

The author

Richard Knight read music at St. John's College, Oxford, and has been Director of Music at two leading independent schools. He now combines teaching with a position as a senior examiner with one of the A level boards and is also on the examiner panel for the ABRSM. He has written several books for Rhinegold Education including study guides for GCSE, AS and A2 levels. Richard is also a composer with a diverse range of works to his name, including opera, oratorio and chamber music.

Acknowledgements

The author would like to thank the Rhinegold editorial and design team for their expert support in the preparation of this book.

Copyright

Companion website and audio

Throughout the book you will see the following icon:

This icon means there is audio available on the book's companion website to accompany the exercise. Go to www.hybridpublications.com and enter the code EK193 which will unlock the content to support this book. The numbers in the icons relate to the track numbers on the website.

You'll also find scores here to help you with the specimen questions.

Some of the exercises require you to access a piece of music. Rhinegold Education have created a YouTube playlist of the recommended clips. You'll see a YouTube icon next to these exercises, with clip number to help you find it in the playlist. Links to the videos are available on the website, or access the playlist here:

http://tinyurl.com/7scb28g

Introduction and about the exam

In order to gain your AS in music with AQA, you will need to complete the following sections:

■ Unit 1: Influences on Music (worth 30% of total AS marks)
■ Unit 2: Composing: Creating Musical Ideas (worth 30% of total AS marks)
■ Unit 3: Performing: Interpreting Musical Ideas (worth 40% of total AS marks).

The focus of this revision guide will primarily be on Unit 1. In particular, you will find:

■ Material to help you prepare for the listening questions in Section A
■ Analytical information on the set work in a special revision format for Section B
■ Revision notes on music relevant to each of the various options in Section C
■ Advice on how to write good essays for questions you will answer in Sections B and C.

Also in this book you will find advice on making final preparations for submitting your composition in Unit 2.

Finally, there is some help for candidates approaching their Unit 3 performance.

Remember: your final result does not only reflect how musical, intelligent and enthusiastic you are; a large factor is how well you have done what the examiners want you to do. There are no marks available for the fantastic performance you gave in a concert at Christmas, or how many books about your set work you have read, or how many hours of listening to the music in your chosen Area of Study 2 you have put in over the past 6 months. The examiners can only give marks for how well you have done the tasks required of you in the specification, and they can only do this according to their published mark schemes.

This book is intended to help you to access as many of those marks as your other skills allow, and not trip up over the business of taking the exam.

Good luck!

Top ten tips

1. PLAN YOUR USE OF TIME

Units 2 and 3 have the same deadline for submitting your work: 15 May. Your Unit 1 exam could be as little as a week after this. You will also have other subjects to think about at this very intense time. You do not want to leave all your revision to the last moment.

2. REGULARLY TRAIN YOUR EAR

Half of the marks on the Unit 1 paper are available in Section A: the listening questions. It is very unlikely you will do well if you leave preparing for this to the last minute: the relevant parts of your body (your ears and brain) need training. A sprinter would spend many weeks getting into shape before an important 100m race; you need to be listening to, and thinking about, music every day over a long period of time before you sit this exam. Remember that listening is not the same as hearing. Having music on in the background while you are thinking about something else is hearing; listening means you are concentrating solely on the sounds reaching your ears.

3. LISTEN TO A WIDE RANGE OF MUSIC

The examiners have a huge range of music that they can draw on for Section A questions. In the 2009–2011 papers there were questions based on music by Handel, Haydn, Mozart, Schubert, Mendelssohn, Tchaikovsky, Grieg, Fauré, Stravinsky, Poulenc, Dave Brubeck and Art Pepper. The more you listen to (not just hear) music across a similarly wide range of styles, the less chance there is that you could be caught out in the exam by something unfamiliar to you.

4. LISTEN REGULARLY TO YOUR SET WORK

You will be doing lots of analytical study of your set work, which is important, but – ultimately – music is an aural experience and you should be making yourself fully familiar with the musical experience of listening to the two movements of Beethoven's first symphony. Listening to it should help to cement in place your understanding of the analytical detail you have studied, for you will associate theory with the sound and musical effect.

5. USE YOUR INSTRUMENTAL SKILLS TO PLAY YOUR SET WORK

Whatever instrument you play, you can engage with Beethoven's symphony practically. If you are very fortunate you will play in an orchestra that can read through the two movements during a rehearsal; but even if this experience is not available to you, you can play or sing some part of it somehow. Pianists might like to explore the various arrangements available at http://imslp.org, which include versions for piano solo, piano duet and combinations such as flute, violin, cello and piano. Other instrumentalists or singers can play (or sing) along to the recording, following an appropriate line. Even percussionists can gain from playing the rhythms of the important themes as they come along. The combination of reading the notation with the concentration required to play the music whilst hearing the resulting sounds is a tremendous boost to your brain that has to cope with the challenge of assimilating all the information about this piece.

6. READ YOUR SCORE IN SILENCE, JUST LIKE A BOOK

As you sit reading this revision guide it is not necessary for you to be reading it aloud: the words make sense to your eyes, and – should you wish – you can imagine the sound of someone saying the words out loud as you read. The same should be true for your reading of the musical score. If you have listened (not heard) to the symphony played often enough, you should be able to read the musical score and imagine inside your head the sound of the music being played. This is a huge advantage when you are sat in silence in the exam room writing an essay about the music. Let your eyes follow the score at the tempo of the music, and enjoy your own personal performance inside your mind!

7. ORGANISE YOUR ANALYTICAL INFORMATION INTO CATEGORIES

There is a big danger in Section B that you will include in your essay lots of good information that is not relevant to the question that the examiners have asked. Be methodical: you need to be able to cover each section of the two movements: the introduction, exposition, development, recapitulation and coda. You also need to be able to focus on whichever aspect(s) the question demands: melody, rhythm, harmony and tonality, texture, instrumentation and structure. Organise your revision notes accordingly.

8. WHICHEVER AREA OF STUDY 2 YOU HAVE DONE, APPLY TIPS 5–7 AND LEARN SOME RELEVANT MUSICAL QUOTES

There is absolutely no point spending time writing out quotes in Section B: the examiners know you have a score in the exam room, so just refer to bar numbers. However, in Section C, providing pertinent musical quotes on the manuscript paper that is provided makes a good impression. It is also a much more musical skill than learning bar numbers!

9. MAKE SURE YOUR WRITTEN SUBMISSION FOR UNIT 2 SHOWS YOU HAVE TAKEN CARE

The composing unit does not just rely on how your work sounds: the quality of the written score or annotation makes a big impression on the examiner. It is usually more important than the recording. If you are doing Brief A, check thoroughly for errors such as parallel 5ths or missing 3rds, and make sure that your score for question 2 is well edited with tempo and performance markings. If you are doing Brief B or C, make sure your musical intentions are clear, that you have communicated the musical character of your work and that the material you are providing allows the examiner to follow the recording with the most helpful score or annotation that you can provide.

10. MAKE SURE YOUR RECORDING FOR UNIT 3 IS AS PRECISE AS POSSIBLE

No matter how vibrant the atmosphere in the room when you perform, or (for those taking the alternative options) how advanced your IT is, the moderator will only have the audio recording to assess your work. Make sure it does you justice!

Unit 1 – an overview

Content

Unit 1 is tested through a written examination. This lasts for 1 hour and 45 minutes and comes in **three** sections:

SECTION A: LISTENING

Four questions based on excerpts of unprepared music with short-answer questions, the answers for which are available through careful listening to the music, drawing on your general musical knowledge.

SECTION B: AREA OF STUDY 1

Two essay questions on the compulsory Beethoven first symphony set work will be on the exam paper; you only have to answer **one.**

SECTION C: AREA OF STUDY 2

For each of the three options for this Area of Study there will be two essay questions (making six in all): you only have to answer **one.**

Taking the exam

Your exam will start with the listening section. This involves extracts of music being played out loud in the exam room. The invigilators will have a CD and, as the exam starts, one of the invigilators will press 'play'.

The next half-hour (approximately) of the exam is governed by the CD. After the initial announcement on the CD there will be a silence of 3 minutes in which you can read the question paper. In this time:

- ■ You **should** read the questions for Section A carefully. You may like to highlight any key words in the questions to help you focus your listening on the important points.
- ■ You **could** look ahead to the essay questions for Sections B and C. You might be able to select the title for one of the essays you will be writing and spend some of this time jotting down some sense of an essay plan.
- ■ **Do not** go into a trance and just wait for the next instruction from the voice on the CD.

The music for each question will be played two, three or four times. This will be stated on the question paper and announced on the CD at the start of each question.

When the final playing for the music of the final question in Section A has finished, there will be approximately 1 hour 15 minutes of the exam left for you to write your two essays (one in Section B, the other in Section C). You therefore need to be prepared to write your best essay answers in about 35 minutes per question.

Make sure you keep an eye on the time, and do not spend an hour on the first essay.

You may answer Section C first, should you wish.

Unit 1 - Section A: Listening

The listening section tests both your aural perception and your technical knowledge of musical language. AQA provide a list of terms that you should know and be able to recognise; this can be found on page 5 of the specification. Some of these terms are unlikely to occur in the listening questions (for instance, the terms listed under 'form': these are very difficult to incorporate into aural perception tests); in addition, some other rudimentary terms may be needed in the exam.

> **NOTE**
>
> Your teacher may have a hard copy of the specification you can use; alternatively, it is easy to find online at www.aqa.org.uk.

Definitions for these terms can be found in the Glossary on page 94 of this book. To help you revise, here are a series of exercises for each category (rhythm, melody, harmony, etc.). These are followed by some specimen questions on page 19 that you can do using recordings available online (see Note at the bottom of this page).

> **NOTE**
>
> The exercises are not necessarily AS-style questions, but are designed to improve the focus of your listening and sharpen your understanding of terminology. The specimen questions from page 19 onwards are in more of an AS style.

Exercises

RHYTHM

Rhythm is the fundamental aspect of most styles of music. We often 'feel' it, but we need to apply conscious thought to it in order to 'listen' to it. The following exercises are designed to help you recognise the following terms:

augmentation, diminution, additive rhythm, dotted rhythm, triplet, syncopation, hemiola, accelerando, ritenuto.

> **NOTE**
>
> Go to www.hybridpublications.com and enter the code EK193, which will unlock the supplementary resources for this book. All the audio for these exercises indicated with the following icon are given there.
>
> ◀))
>
> The answers and comments to the exercises can be found from pages 62–79.

◀)) 1 EXERCISE 1

Listen to the rhythm being played in Track 1. Then answer the following questions:

a.   What metre (or time signature) is the rhythm in?
b.   How many bars long is the rhythm?
c.   Identify two bars that have an identical rhythm to each other.
d.   What is the relationship between bars 1–2 and bar 3?
e.   What rhythmic device is used in bar 4?
f.   Which technique affects the rhythm towards the end?

◀)) 2 EXERCISE 2

Listen to the rhythm being played in Track 2. Then answer the following questions:

a.   What metre (or time signature) is the rhythm in?
b.   How many bars long is the rhythm?
c.   On which beat of the bar does the rhythm start?
d.   What type of rhythmic figure is used in bar 3?
e.   What type of rhythmic figure is used at the start of the second half of bars 5 and 6?
f.   What rhythmic device is used in bars 7 and 8?

◀)) 3 EXERCISE 3

Listen to the rhythm being played in Track 3. Then answer the following questions:

a.   What metre (or time signature) is the rhythm in?
b.   How many beats are there in each bar?
c.   How many notes occur before the first barline?
d.   What note value is the first note?
e.   Which bar has the fewest notes in it?
f.   What technique affects the rhythm towards the end?

◀)) 4 EXERCISE 4

Listen to the rhythm being played in Track 4. Then answer the following questions:

a.   What kind of metre is being used here to give a lively feel?
b.   How many beats are there in each bar?
c.   What is unusual about the fourth beat of each bar?
d.   How many bars in total are there?
e.   How do bars 5 and 6 differ from bars 1 and 2?

MELODY

Melody is often the most obvious aspect of music to listen to, as it is usually at the top of the texture and tends to be the part of a piece that we remember best after the music is played.

The next set of exercises are designed to help you recognise the following terms:

conjunct, disjunct, triadic, blue notes, diatonic, scalic, pentatonic, whole tone, sequence, inversion, glissando.

The exercises also should help you to recognise melodic intervals and various ornaments.

◀)) 5 EXERCISE 5

Listen to the melody being played in Track 5. Then answer the following questions:

a. Is the melody in a major or minor key?
b. Which two words best describe the contour of the opening four bars of the melody?
c. Which of these two words does not apply to the next phrase (bars 5–6)?
d. What other word might now be used to describe bars 5–6?
e. How does the final phrase (bars 7–8) differ from the rest of the melody?
f. Does the final phrase share a characteristic with bars 1–4 or bars 5–6?
g. What type of ornament occurs twice during the course of the melody?

◀)) 6 EXERCISE 6

Listen to the melody being played in Track 6. Then answer the following questions:

a. Is the melody in a major or minor key?
b. Which word best describes the contour of the first half of the melody?
c. What direction does the melody move in during the first six bars?
d. How does the contour change at bar 7?
e. What ornament decorates the melody near to the end?
f. What is the interval between the final two notes?

◀)) 7 EXERCISE 7

Listen to the melody being played in Track 7. Then answer the following questions:

a. How many phrases make up this melody?
b. What is the relationship of the second phrase to the first phrase?
c. What is the relationship of the second half of the melody to the first half?
d. What kind of scale has been used to compose this melody?

🔊 8 EXERCISE 8

Listen to the melody being played in Track 8. Then answer the following questions:

a. What elements give the melody and rhythm a strong jazz character in the opening four bars?

b. What device is used in the melody in bar 4?

c. How does the melodic contour differ in the central phrase from what is heard previously? Give three differences.

d. What special playing technique is used for the final note of the melody?

MELODIC DICTATION PRACTICE

One of the questions in Section A is likely to require you to fill in missing notes in a melodic phrase. It may only be four notes that are needed to fill the gap, but with a mark for each note, this seemingly insignificant question is actually 10% of the Section A marks. It is therefore well worth careful, patient practice.

🔊 9–16 EXERCISE 9

The following melody (page 14) is missing its notes for bar 3. There are eight different versions of the bar, which you can hear in Tracks 9–16. In each case there are four notes in the empty bar; the rhythm is always two quavers plus two crotchets.

Listen to each version **three** times and fill in the missing notes.

NOTE

There are three factors to consider:

- The link from the last note of bar 2 to the first missing note – is it the same, lower or higher in pitch?
- The shape of the melodic contour in bar 3 – rising or falling, conjunct or disjunct?
- The link from the last note you write in bar 3 to the written note in bar 4 – the same, lower or higher in pitch?

You may like to consider one factor on each hearing.

This skill offers a great opportunity for teamwork revision: write your own four-bar phrase (keep it simple!) with different versions of the third bar and then challenge a fellow student to work out the various contours you play to him or her.

Then get ready to deal with the return favour!

(a)

(b)

(c)

(d)

(e)

(f)

(g)

(h)

HARMONY

We now move on to consider aspects of harmony that you may be required to spot aurally in Section A. Often harmony requires, quite literally, a deeper level of listening. Whereas the rhythm and melody are frequently heard on the surface – the top strand of the texture – harmony is usually governed by the bass line and formed by the notes in the middle of the texture. However, it is this very depth to which harmony reaches that often makes it one of the most profound and expressive elements in music. Training the ear to hear harmony is therefore a way to appreciate music more richly.

The next set of exercises are designed to help you recognise the following harmonic features:

> consonant, dissonant, major, minor, modal, passing note, auxiliary note, appoggiatura, suspension, pedal note, cadences, tierce de Picardie, modulation, harmonic rhythm.

◄))17 EXERCISE 10

Listen to the music in Track 17. Then answer the following questions:

a. What word best describes the tonality of the music?
b. What type of note decorates the third chord of the piece?
c. What kind of cadence occurs halfway through at the end of the first phrase?
d. What kind of note decorates the first chord of the second phrase?
e. What kind of cadence ends the piece? Identify the final three chords.
f. Does the music end in the same key as it started in?

◄))18 EXERCISE 11

Listen to the music in Track 18. Then answer the following questions:

a. What word best describes the tonality of this music?
b. What harmonic device is heard at the start?
c. A similar device occurs at the start of the second phrase. How is it different this time?
d. Does the music end in the same key as it started in?
e. What cadence occurs at the end of the piece?
f. What device is used in the final chord?

◄))19 EXERCISE 12

Listen to the music in Track 19. Then answer the following questions:

a. What word best describes the first chord you hear? (The second chord, two bars later, is the same chord but an octave lower.)
b. What harmonic pattern underpins the main melody that comes after the four-bar introduction?
c. What kind of cadence finishes the main section (i.e. just before the silent pause)?
d. The music begins in C major. In which key does it finish?
e. What kind of cadence comes at the very end?

◄))20 EXERCISE 13

Listen to the music in Track 20. Then answer the following questions:

a. What word best describes the tonality of this music?
b. How does the note in the melody decorate the first chord? (The third, fifth and seventh chords are all decorated in a similar way.)
c. What is significant about how the harmony changes in the third phrase?
d. How is the final chord decorated?

TEXTURE

Many people find the vocabulary for texture challenging to use, but the differences in texture that exist in music are usually fairly clear to hear. The following exercise should help you to identify textures that are:

> homophonic, contrapuntal, melody with accompaniment, antiphonal, fugal and canonic.

The exercises also incorporate other issues already met in this chapter.

◀))21 EXERCISE 14

Listen to the music in Track 21. Then answer the following questions:

a. What is the best description of the texture of this piece?
b. What change occurs in the texture for the second phrase?
c. What is the interval between the first two notes of the melody? Phrases 2 and 3 both begin with the same interval.
d. What ornament occurs during the melody in the second phrase?
e. What type of cadence comes at the end of the third phrase (which is the penultimate phrase)?
f. What type of cadence finishes the piece?

◀))22 EXERCISE 15

Listen to the music in Track 22. Then answer the following questions:

a. What is the best description of the texture of this piece?
b. What word best describes the tonality of the piece?
c. What is significant about the texture halfway through the piece, when the dynamic changes to *f*?
d. What type of cadence finishes the piece?
e. What type of ornament is used in the melody during the final cadence?
f. What type of ornament is used on the final note of the piece (in the bass)?

◀))23 EXERCISE 16

Listen to the music in Track 23. Then answer the following questions:

a. What is the best description of the texture of this piece?
b. What word best describes the tonality of the piece?
c. The music begins in F major; in which key does it finish?
d. What is the metre (time signature) of the music?
e. What rhythmic device is used at the end?
f. What type of cadence finishes the piece?

◀))24 EXERCISE 17

Listen to the music in Track 24. Then answer the following questions:

a. What is the best description of the texture of this piece?
b. What is the metre of the music?
c. What rhythmic device is used after the first phrase?
d. What melodic and harmonic device is used in the second half?
e. The music starts in A♭ major; in which key does it finish?
f. What device is used in the final chord?

◀))25 EXERCISE 18

Listen to the music in Track 25. Then answer the following questions:

a. What is the best description of the texture of this piece?
b. How many times during the course of the piece do you hear the opening melodic idea played?
c. What is significant about the way this melodic idea is played on its last appearance (in the bass just before the end)?
d. What is the tonality of the piece?
e. What type of cadence finishes the piece?
f. What device decorates the final chord?

◀))26 EXERCISE 19

Listen to the music in Track 26. Then answer the following questions:

a. Which **two** words describe the texture of this piece?
b. What harmonic progression underpins the passage of longer legato phrases in the middle of the piece?
c. When the opening theme returns near the end, how is it different from before?

INSTRUMENTATION AND TIMBRE

It is very likely that some of the Section A marks will be for identifying some aspects of instrumentation in the excerpts you hear. Often this involves orchestral music.

If you have played for years in an orchestra, this should be very straightforward. If not, the only way to be sure of securing these marks is to have enough experience of orchestral music. It cannot be done through reading a book or making copious revision notes.

So try to attend some orchestral concerts. Exam preparation never gets more enjoyable than this! It need not be expensive. A number of top-class performance venues often sell standby tickets to students for as little as £5.

If you live too far from a concert hall for this to be a possibility, and you need to improve your recognition of instrumental timbres from home, then no one can help you better than

Benjamin Britten and his *Variations and Fugue on a Theme of Purcell*, better known as *The Young Person's Guide to the Orchestra*. You can find it in Rhinegold Education's YouTube playlist for this book in two parts:

Part 1 at: **You Tube 1**

Part 2 at: **You Tube 2**

Here, you can link the sounds with the instruments you see on screen. Then concentrate on just listening and make sure you know which instrument is which.

NOTE

Britten starts with the full orchestral sound and then skilfully deconstructs it into instrumental families (strings, woodwinds, brass, percussion). Next he goes through each family a second time, introducing each member with its own variation. Finally he puts the orchestra back together, instrument by instrument, in a dazzling fugue – starting with the piccolo.

When listening to the work, don't just concentrate on the leading instrument(s) for each variation: listen to the accompaniment too and work out what is being used to support each star turn. Britten's orchestration is highly skilled in this way too.

You Tube 3 **EXERCISE 20**

This exercise is a test of your ability to identify woodwind and brass instruments in an orchestral piece.

First, listen to the recording of the third movement (Adagio) of Rachmaninov's second symphony conducted by Vladimir Ashkenazy. This is available on YouTube (audio only).

Listen to the first two-and-a-half minutes: there is a very beautiful and long clarinet solo, and – at the start – this arched figure is heard in the violins:

You may wish to take the time to listen to the whole movement (the climax midway is well worth it), but this exercise now moves to the recapitulation much later in the movement.

 For this access the fourth clip in the YouTube playlist and the passage starting at 1:13.

Here the long melody that was played before by the solo clarinet is now played by the first violins, and around it the original violin figure is played 11 times before the long theme is completed at 3:16. Listen carefully, and note down which instrument plays the arched figure each of the 11 times it appears.

In actual fact the arch motif occurs throughout much of the movement, and there are plenty of other appearances of it elsewhere for you to spot the instrument (including some not covered in the above exercise), so you can enjoy the whole movement!

Instrumentation and timbre is a vast topic, and a book of this scope can only give you a few pointers: it is up to you to gain the real-life experience of how each instrument sounds to you. It is not unlike learning the names we give to colours: quite how would you teach someone the difference between red and orange, blue and purple, without actually showing them the colours? So you need to listen (not just hear) as much instrumental music as possible.

In particular, listen for:

- Orchestras: the different instruments and playing techniques ranging from mutes (strings and brass) to flutter-tonguing (woodwinds) and pizzicato and col legno (strings).
- Jazz ensembles: the various different kinds of saxophones, bass instruments, drumkit sounds and specialist trumpet and trombone mutes.
- Pop music: different guitar effects and the sounds generated and edited electronically.
- Singers: different voice types from coloratura soprano to contralto and countertenor to bass, and specialist singing techniques such as scat singing.

Revising this section should be pure fun!

Specimen questions

There are usually two types of question in Section A.

- Questions 1–3 are similar: essentially purely aural, short-answer questions. One of the questions will probably include notation for part of the melody with some notes missing that you have to fill in (as on page 14). It is possible that one of the questions might involve two different pieces of music being played to you.
- Question 4 is usually different. You will still hear the music played, but there will also be a score of the music, which in the past has been an orchestral piece. This allows the examiners to ask more location-specific questions and will test your skills for score-reading, including handling transposing instruments.

The answers and comments to the specimen questions can be found on pages 80–83.

FOUR 'AURAL ONLY' QUESTIONS

Suggested recordings from YouTube are provided in Rhinegold Education's YouTube playlist, as well as advice on locating the correct passage from other sources. You should play the excerpts the number of times stated in the questions, with a gap of 20 seconds between each playing.

QUESTION 1

You will hear an excerpt from Mozart's *Kegelstatt Trio* K. 498. The music will be played four times with pauses between each playing.

a. Which string instrument plays with the piano at the start? *(1 mark)*
b. Which ornament features as part of the main motif that is heard many times: acciaccatura, mordent, trill or turn? *(1 mark)*
c. Which wind instrument enters in bar 9? *(1 mark)*
d. What kind of scale does this instrument play at the end of its first phrase? *(2 marks)*
e. What is the tonality of this music? *(1 mark)*
f. A second theme is introduced by the wind instrument after two slow piano chords. What key is this theme played in: dominant, relative major, relative minor or subdominant? *(1 mark)*
g. What is the best description of the texture of this new section: canonic, contrapuntal, homophonic, or melody with accompaniment? *(1 mark)*
h. What cadence is heard at the end of the excerpt? *(1 mark)*
i. Give a suitable time signature for the piece. *(1 mark)*

Total: 10 marks

QUESTION 2

You will hear an excerpt from Malcolm Arnold's *English Dances* Set 2, No. 3, 'Grazioso'. The music will be played four times with pauses between each playing.

a. The music is built over a repeating pattern of two chords. Which percussion instrument is involved with the chords? *(1 mark)*
b. What is the interval between the bass notes of the chords: 3rd, 4th, 5th or 6th? *(1 mark)*

c. Complete the empty bar in the oboe melody by filling in the four missing quavers.
(4 marks)

d. Which instruments play the melody after the oboe? *(2 marks)*

e. The strings then take over the melody. How is the texture different at this point? *(1 mark)*

f. What is the tonality of the music? *(1 mark)*

Total: 10 marks

QUESTION 3

You will hear an excerpt from a sonata by César Franck. The music will be played four times with pauses between each playing.

NOTE

Recommended recording (with Jascha Heifitz and Arthur Rubinstein):

You Tube ▸ 7

Stop at 0:55.

If you are listening to a recording from a different source, it is the opening of the fourth movement of the sonata (Allegretto ben moderato) up to bar 37.

a. What is the solo instrument that the piano is accompanying? *(1 mark)*

b. How is the instrument being played: arco, col legno, pizzicato or sul ponticello? *(1 mark)*

c. Complete the first phrase of the melody below by filling in the missing notes. *(4 marks)*

d. Which **one** of the following best describes the melody at the start: chromatic, diatonic, pentatonic or whole tone? *(1 mark)*

e. What is the texture of the music: canonic, fugal, heterophonic, or melody with accompaniment? *(1 mark)*

f. What cadence is heard at the end of the excerpt? *(1 mark)*

g. Which **one** of the following statements is true? *(1 mark)*
- The music remains in the same key throughout
- The music ends in the dominant key
- The music ends in the same key as it began
- The music ends in the relative minor.

Total: 10 marks

QUESTION 4

You will hear an excerpt from Tchaikovsky's Symphony No. 4. The music will be played four times with pauses between each playing.

NOTE

Recommended recording:

You Tube 8

Stop at 1:35.

If you are listening to a recording from a different source, it is the second movement up to bar 41 (just before figure A).

a. Which instrument plays the melody at the start? *(1 mark)*
b. What term best describes the playing technique heard in the strings? *(1 mark)*
c. What is the tonality of the music? *(1 mark)*
d. The main melody is repeated by part of the string section. Which instruments play it: violins, violas, cellos or double basses? *(1 mark)*
e. At this point there is a countermelody on two clarinets. Which description best fits their phrase? *(1 mark)*
- A rising arpeggio in unison
- A rising arpeggio in octaves
- A rising scale in unison
- A rising scale in octaves.
f. The countermelody then passes to another woodwind instrument. Which instrument? *(1 mark)*
g. Which **three** of the following can be heard in the excerpt? *(3 marks)*
- Circle of 5ths harmony
- Hemiola
- Imperfect cadence
- Ostinato
- Plagal cadence
- Sequence
- Tierce de Picardie.

h. Give a suitable time signature. *(1 mark)*

Total: 10 marks

TWO 'WITH SCORE' QUESTIONS

Scores for these questions are provided on the book companion website at www.hybridpublications.com.

QUESTION 5

You will hear an excerpt from the third movement of Haydn's Symphony No. 89. The music will be played twice with a pause between the playings.

NOTE

Recommended recording:

You Tube 9

Stop at 1:31.

If you are listening to a recording from a different source, it is the Menuet section of the third movement, stopping where the Trio starts.

a. Complete this sentence to describe the texture in the opening four-bar phrase: "There is a _ _ _ _ _-part texture doubled at _ _ _ _ _ _ different octaves. *(2 marks)*
b. What compositional technique does Haydn use in bars 4^3 to 6^2? *(1 mark)*
c. In what key does the music cadence at bar 12? *(1 mark)*
d. What harmonic device is used in bars 8–12? *(1 mark)*
e. Which instruments continue this device in bars 13–16? *(2 marks)*
f. At what interval apart are the violas and cellos between bars 28^3 and 31^1: 2nd, 3rd, 5th or 6th? *(1 mark)*
g. Give a bar and beat number where the first horn sounds higher than the first oboe for the duration of the entire beat. *(1 mark)*
h. In what form is this excerpt: binary, rondo, sonata or ternary? *(1 mark)*

Total: 10 marks

QUESTION 6

You will hear an excerpt from the first movement of Reicha's Wind Quintet in C major Op. 91 No. 1. The music will be played three times with a pause between the playings.

a. What ornament does the oboe play in bars 4 and 6? *(1 mark)*
b. Describe fully the chord marked *X* in bar 8. *(2 marks)*
c. Describe fully the chord marked *Y* in bar 8. *(2 marks)*
d. What key does the music change to for the Andante section? *(1 mark)*
e. What harmonic progression occurs in bars 18–21? *(1 mark)*
f. What ornament does the flute play in bar 25? *(1 mark)*
g. What interval apart are the flute and clarinet in bars 34–35? *(1 mark)*
h. Identify a bar in which the horn sounds lower than the bassoon. *(1 mark)*

Total: 10 marks

Unit 1 – Section B: Historical Study – Area of Study 1 (set work)

This section of the exam is based on your study of the set work: Beethoven's first symphony, movements 1 and 2. It tests your analytical understanding of the music and your ability to write well about the piece, choosing examples from the music that suit a given question, and being able to describe the construction and effect of the music using a suitable technical vocabulary with confidence.

The material here is designed to help you prepare for this section of the exam and comes in two halves:

■ Firstly, there is advice on structuring your revision notes. This provides you with ready examples for some passages of the symphony, and then encourages you to produce similar material for the rest of the two movements set by AQA.

■ Secondly, we look at AQA's mark scheme and look at various examples of answers to some questions in order to gain an examiner's insight into what makes for a good essay style for this exam.

NOTE

Completing your own revision notes will in itself be an excellent way of revising, especially if you follow the examples given below.

Making revision notes

THE AIM

For your set work study, you will have analysed the first and second movements from Beethoven's first symphony.

In the exam there will be two essay questions from which you choose **one** to answer. These questions are numbered 5 and 6 on the exam paper. You will have about 35 minutes to write your essay, which will then be marked out of 20.

It is likely that question 5 will be based on the first movement of the symphony, whilst question 6 will ask something about the second movement. However, make sure you read the question carefully: it is possible that a question could refer to both movements.

Commonly, there are two types of question:

1. Write in detail about one passage of music with reference to all elements of music. For example: *'Write an informative account of the introduction in the first movement of this symphony. You should refer to structure, melody, texture, instrumentation, rhythm, harmony and tonality.'*

2. Write about an entire movement with reference to just one (or maybe two) elements of music. For example: *'Describe the ways in which Beethoven makes use of rhythm in the second movement of this symphony.'*

In either style of question it is easy to be drawn off course. In the first you can find yourself writing about music from elsewhere in the movement; in the second it is easy to spend time writing about elements other than the one set by the question. 35 minutes is not long for writing an answer to either question, and you cannot afford to spend 5 minutes writing a very interesting paragraph about something that lies outside the scope of the question. You will not get any marks for such a paragraph.

In order to be able to practise writing essays of the kind you will need to write in the exam room, it is recommended that you organise your revision notes according to the following tables. In theses tables, the boxes with ticks are those for which example pages can be found below. As you compile your own pages for the other boxes you can tick them; this way you can see at a glance how much there is still to do.

FIRST MOVEMENT

	Introduction	Exposition	Development	Recapitulation	Coda
Structure	✓				
Melody	✓				
Rhythm	✓				
Harmony	✓	✓	✓	✓	✓
Texture	✓				
Instrumentation	✓				

SECOND MOVEMENT

	Exposition	Development	Recapitulation	Coda
Structure				✓
Melody				✓
Rhythm	✓	✓	✓	✓
Harmony				✓
Texture				✓
Instrumentation				✓

To revise with maximum thoroughness, you should aim to have a separate page for each box in the grids. At the top left corner of the page put the section of the movement:

FIRST MOVEMENT: EXPOSITION

and at the top right corner of the page put the element:

INSTRUMENTATION

Then, if you are writing an essay on the first-movement exposition, you can use all the pages with 'First movement: exposition' *and limit yourself to the facts you have on those pages.* Similarly, if you are writing about instrumentation in the second movement, use the relevant sheets as your guide to what to write.

There will not be – necessarily – an equal amount to say for the topic represented by each box. Make sure you only include:

■ Relevant points
■ Good-quality points
■ Points that you fully understand.

NOTE

As a refinement to this system, you may wish to use different-colour paper for the two movements. A third colour could be used for your Section C notes.

This also means that you can revise methodically: concentrating one session on 'Texture' and the next on 'Second movement: exposition', for instance. This way, your revision will look at each page of the score from different angles and be all the more thorough for it.

In the tables above, the boxes with ticks are those for which example pages can be found below. As you compile your own pages for the other boxes you can tick them; this way you can see at a glance how much there is still to do.

EXAMPLE REVISION PAGES: FIRST MOVEMENT

Not every page will have an equal amount of information: there may be more to say about the exposition than the coda, or about melody than texture in some sections. Set out the information spaciously, so it is easy to remember each point at a glance. Make sure important points are linked to a specific example in the score with a bar-number reference.

FIRST MOVEMENT: INTRODUCTION – STRUCTURE

Overview

Like many symphonies by the first master of the symphony, Haydn, the Allegro first movement begins with a slow introduction: in this case 12 bars of Adagio molto.

With an almost Classical sense of proportion, these 12 bars comprise three balanced segments:

Bars 1–4

A series of cadential patterns designed to draw attention to the dominant chord on the downbeat of bar 4.

The chords are bold root positions, but also a little enigmatic: what key are they pointing to?

Bars 5–8

A passage of some suspense created by:

- A softer dynamic
- Dense texture
- Slow-moving, twisting conjunct melody in the violins
- A (decorated) inverted dominant pedal in the oboe and clarinet
- A countermelody in flute and bassoon that starts with a falling triadic shape
- Harmony that – with the exception of the dominant chord – avoids assertive root-position chords.

Bars 8–12

A return to strong homophonic music, though the softer bar 9 includes a significant set of four descending quavers.

The introduction concludes with material in the winds that echoes bars 3–4 and the unequivocal arrival in C major as the *Allegro* starts.

FIRST MOVEMENT: INTRODUCTION – MELODY

Bars 1–4

Melody plays a subsidiary role to the harmonic progression. The top line of the texture repeatedly moves from leading note to tonic in three cadences, each in a different key.

Bars 5–8

The primary melodic line is essentially conjunct, with chromatic inflections in bars 6 and 7.

A countermelody (flute and bassoon, with horns joining in bar 6) uses a falling triadic shape that reflects the linking phrase in the violins in bar 4 (A–F–D).

Bars 8–12

Chords are again more important than melody here. There are significant melodic elements, however:

- The falling four quavers in bar 9 – the first appearance of an important motif
- The rising semitone step at the top of the chords in bar 11 that mirror bars 3–4
- The string scales in bar 12: a rising G major scale – one final moment of obscuring the symphony's tonic key – and then a falling scale down (through an F♯) to the clear keynote of C at the start of the *Allegro*.

FIRST MOVEMENT: INTRODUCTION – RHYTHM

Bars 1–4

There is very little significant rhythmic content at first. In bars 1 and 2, chords change on the first and third beats of the bar.

Bars 5–8

The melody in bars 5–7 has a similar rhythm in each bar with a tie midway and seven semiquavers in the second half of the bar.

The falling triadic shape in the woodwind countermelody in bars 5 and 6 is at half the speed (rhythmic diminution) compared to the first appearance of the motif in the violins in bar 4.

Bars 8–12

The falling four-note figure that first appears in bar 9 as quavers increases to demisemiquavers in bar 12.

FIRST MOVEMENT: INTRODUCTION – HARMONY

Bars 1–4

The remarkable opening is as follows:

bar 1	bar 2	bar 3	bar 4
C^7 → F	G^7 → Am	D^7	G
Perfect cadence in F	Interrupted cadence in C	Perfect cadence in G	

This progression, which on first hearing can seem tonally bewildering, has the effect of emphasising that G is the dominant (and, therefore, that C must be the tonic).

Bars 5–8

There is an internal dominant pedal in the oboe and clarinet (a little decorated at times). Meanwhile, the chords explore various inversions (after the root positions of bars 1–4):

bar 5	bar 6	bar 7	bar 8^1
V → V^{7}d	Ib	Vb → V	I

Bars 8–12

As the introduction finishes, there is a very effective halving of harmonic rhythm:

bar 8	bar 9	bar 10	bar 11	bar 12
I → IIb	Ic → V^7	VI → IV	Ic	V^7

Bars 9–10 threaten to be a perfect cadence but, on the last quaver of bar 9, a chromatic inflection forces it to become an interrupted cadence. The subsequent perfect cadence in bars 11–13 is slower and more conclusive, resolving onto C major as the *Allegro* starts.

FIRST MOVEMENT: INTRODUCTION – TEXTURE

Bars 1–4

Straightforward homophony.

Bars 5–8

A more elaborate polyphonic texture with various strands woven together in a rich orchestral texture.

Bars 8–12

Essentially, a return to homophony, with a touch of antiphony between strings and the rest of the orchestra in bars 8 and 10.

The woodwinds and horns provide a chordal backdrop for the strings in octaves to spin their scales in bar 12.

FIRST MOVEMENT: INTRODUCTION – INSTRUMENTATION

Bars 1–4

Chords are sustained by the wind; their $f\!\!p$ markings are given extra attack through the pizzicato string reinforcement.

Bars 5–8

Considerable colour is given to the orchestration through octave doubling of various lines:

- The melody: doubled in octaves on the violins
- The countermelody: doubled in octaves by flute and bassoon
- The decorated pedal note: doubled in octaves by oboe and clarinet
- A mix of countermelody and pedal note: in octaves on the horns
- The bass line: doubled in octaves by cellos (and second bassoon) and basses.

Bars 8–12

The clearer homophonic texture is given added sparkle with tonic and dominant notes played by trumpets and timpani to complete a full orchestral *tutti*.

FIRST MOVEMENT: EXPOSITION – HARMONY

First subject

There is a very slow-moving progression of:

   I (bar 13) → II (bar 19) → V (bar 25) → I (bar 31)

massaged by chromatic inflections in bar 18 and bar 24.

This is followed by a fast-moving cadential pattern of:

   I (bar 31¹) → IV (bar 31²) → Ic (bar 32¹) → V7 (bar 32²) → I (bar 33)

The next eight-bar phrase is harmonised with I and V⁷ over a tonic pedal.

Transition

Four bars of a melodic line doubled in octaves (bars 41–44) imply a rising harmonic pattern with secondary 7ths:

bar 41[1]	bar 41[2]	bar 42[1]	bar 42[2]	bar 43
C	A^7	Dm	B^7	Em
I	V^7 of...	II	V^7 of...	III

Greater momentum in the pattern in bar 44 lifts the music to G, whereupon there are eight bars with a pedal G (punctuated by the timpani) over which alternate chords of G and C (second inversion).

Second subject

The second subject is presented – as expected – in the dominant key of G major.

The first eight-bar phrase of the second subject is based on diatonic chords:

bar 53	bar 54	bar 55	bar 56	bar 57	bar 58	bar 59	bar 60
I	V^7c	V^7	I	$V/V^7b \rightarrow I$	$V/V^7b \rightarrow I$	$Vc \rightarrow V^7$ of V	V

In an answering phrase there are two diminished 7th chords that are enharmonically equivalent (sound the same) but are notated differently because they have different functions:

- End of bar 65   B, D, F, A♭ G^{-9} = V of...   C in bar 66
- End of bar 66   B, D, F, G♯ E^{-9} = V of...   Am in bar 67

After a very confident G major passage from bar 69 there is a sudden change to G minor at bar 77. This allows for a different palette of chords (lots of flats) to be used, which Beethoven explores in a circle of 5ths progression:

bar 77	bar 78	bar 79	bar 80	bar 81
G minor	C minor	F^7	B♭ major	E♭ major

The route home to G major is via D^7 in bar 85: the dominant 7th of both G minor and G major.

There are rich harmonic moments in the final phrase: three diminished 7th chords in bars 93, 95 and 97. Each operates as a dominant minor 9th to the following chord.

Codetta

Simple harmony here comprises only chords I and V^7 (in G major).

FIRST MOVEMENT: DEVELOPMENT – HARMONY

The G^7 descending arpeggio in the winds at the end of the exposition naturally wants to resolve back to C major (as it does when the exposition is repeated); however, a progression a little like an interrupted cadence moves onto a surprising A major chord: a clear signal that the development has begun.

Bars 110–136

The first section of the development is built on a *falling* circle of 5ths progression, each harmony being present for a four-bar phrase:

bars 110–113	bars 114–117	bars 118–121	bars 122–125	bars 126–129	bars 130–136
A major	D major	G major	C minor	F minor	B♭ pedal

In the first three of these phrases, the harmony gradually evolves from a major triad into a dominant 7th and then a dominant minor 9th, thereby gathering the momentum to move on to the next chord.

The use of minor chords for the chords on C and F (involving various flats) enables Beethoven to rapidly move towards a new, distant tonal centre. The progression heard above the B♭ pedal in bars 130–136…

bars 130–131	bars 132–133	bars 134–135	bar 136
B♭ major	E♭ major	F^{-9}	B♭ major

…identifies B♭ as being significant to that new tonal centre – not as its tonic, but as its dominant. It is similar to the start of the movement, where the importance of G at bar 4 is emphasised because it is going to be the dominant of the whole symphony.

Bars 136–160

Having drawn attention to B♭ in the previous *ff* passage, Beethoven now cements its role as a dominant with eight bars built from B♭^{7}–E♭ harmony – in other words V^7–I in E♭ major.

The long B♭ preparation makes the arrival of E♭ major in bar 144 seem like the most significant tonal centre used in the development. Its relationship to the original tonic – the flattened mediant – is one often associated with Beethoven.

After the falling harmonic pattern that started the development, Beethoven now uses a *rising* pattern in order to have a sense of building tension to be released at the *ff* moment of recapitulation. Note the quickening harmonic rhythm:

bar 144	bar 148	bar 152	bar 156	bar 158	bar 160
4 bars	4 bars	4 bars	2 bars	2 bars	new section
E♭	F minor	G minor	D minor	A minor	E
	Rising steps				
			Rising 5ths→		

The prominence of dark minor keys here emphasises that this is the middle of a movement that started – and is expected to end – in bright C major. It makes the arrival of C major when the recapitulation comes all the more resplendent.

Bars 160–177

The note E is all-important here (played by horns and trumpets) and supports harmony of E^7 and A minor. Beethoven is keeping the brightness of the imminent return to C major hidden by approaching it from its relative minor (which, of course, has the same key signature). Eventually (bar 174) he reaches up a semitone to begin a dominant 7th falling arpeggio, and the recapitulation is soon unleashed.

FIRST MOVEMENT: RECAPITULATION – HARMONY

First subject

This section takes the same harmonic progression as in the exposition until it is abbreviated after 12 bars (at bar 190).

Transition

As is usual, the transition in the recapitulation is rewritten, and Beethoven seizes on the potential for a dramatic passage of building excitement. The harmony is an ascending progression, each rising step prefaced by its own dominant 7th.

Initially this is in semibreves (one chord per bar)…

bar 188	bar 189	bar 190	bar 191	bar 192
D	C^7 (V of…)	F	D^7 (V of…)	G

…and then, with a doubling of harmonic rhythm, in minims:

bar 192	bar 193	bar 194	bar 195	bar 196	bar 197	bar 198
G → E^7	Am → F^7	B♭ → G^7	C → A^7	Dm → C^7	F → D^7	G

After this harmonic excitement, the transition ends with eight bars of a dominant pedal ready for the first appearance of the second subject in C major.

Second subject

This section follows the same course and harmony as in the exposition, except that it is now in *C major*. Therefore, the passage that was first heard in G minor at bar 77, now appears in C minor at bar 230.

Codetta

Likewise, this too is similar to the equivalent passage in the exposition, other than it is in the tonic key.

FIRST MOVEMENT: CODA – HARMONY

Bars 259–271

Just when an emphatic perfect cadence has concluded the recapitulation firmly in C major, Beethoven engages in a little teasing in the coda.

This is achieved through some prolonged secondary 7th chords:

bars 260–262	bar 263	bars 264–266	bar 267	bars 268–270	bar 271
C^7 (V of…)	F	A^7 (V of…)	Dm	G^7 (V of…)	C

Bars 271–277

In a strong *tutti* homophonic passage Beethoven tries three times to find a conclusive perfect cadence. Twice he side-steps via a G♯ in the bass into an interrupted cadence; the third time there is no alternative but chord I and a resounding perfect cadence.

Bars 277–298

The movement ends with a long and stable passage using only a tonic (chord I) harmony.

EXAMPLE REVISION PAGES: SECOND MOVEMENT

SECOND MOVEMENT: EXPOSITION – RHYTHM

First subject

The triple-time metre suggests a sense of dance, and the anacrusis enhances the lilt of the music. This is underlined by the bowing detail.

The dotted pattern, first heard in bar 3, is destined to be a very important element of the movement.

sf markings – typical of Beethoven – occur on the weaker beats from bar 20.

Second subject

The greater delicacy present in the first half of the second subject is partly due to rhythmic factors:

- The first subject's dotted rhythm pattern is now used as an anacrusis
- Demisemiquavers are used for a turn figure in bar 23
- Elsewhere, even semiquavers permeate the texture
- Dotted rhythms become very important in the second half of the second subject (from bar 42)
- *sf* markings stress the second beat of the bar in bars 49–51.

Codetta

The dotted rhythm idea is taken on by the timpani.

Meanwhile, flute and first violins have a long line of dainty triplet semiquavers.

SECOND MOVEMENT: DEVELOPMENT – RHYTHM

Bars 65–81

The two main ideas here are:

- The rhythmic identity of anacrusis plus downbeat that sets the movement going at the start
- The dotted rhythm pattern (from bar 71).

Bars 81–100

The dotted rhythm pattern is maintained by the timpani.

Repetitions of the anacrusis-plus-downbeat idea continue, but now following on immediately, one pair of quavers after another, creating a hemiola effect (from bar 85).

SECOND MOVEMENT: RECAPITULATION – RHYTHM

First subject

This is essentially the same as in the exposition.

A new element is provided by the countermelody in running semiquavers, initially in the cellos and then the violins.

Second subject

This has the same rhythmic content as in the exposition. Note the second-beat *sf* markings in bars 149–151.

Codetta

This has the same rhythmic content as in the exposition. The dotted rhythms are again carried by the timpani.

SECOND MOVEMENT: CODA – STRUCTURE

Bars 163–170

The coda starts with a restatement of the opening phrase to the first subject.

Bars 170–182

The second half of the phrase just played is extended and treated to something of a mini-development involving a variety of tonal centres.

Bars 182–190

Tonal stability (in the tonic of F major) returns, but the texture is built on the dotted rhythms in a manner reminiscent of the main development, whilst the melody is based on and extends bar 3 of the first subject.

Bars 190–195

A simple series of four perfect cadences, the last one a feigning of a *f* ending, followed by three *p* tonic chords.

SECOND MOVEMENT: CODA – MELODY

Bars 163–170

A restatement of the opening phrase of the first subject, comprising:

- A rising tonic triad (C–F–A)
- A falling F major scale (B♭ down to E)
- A rising F major scale (E up to C).

Bars 170–182

The final rising scale from the previous phrase is then repeated in G minor as a rising sequence.

A further varied repetition follows, starting in B♭ major.

Bars 182–190

In the first violins, a rising 7th precedes a falling F major scale of an octave and a 4th.

This is repeated in conjunction with a rising scale in the flute.

Bars 190–195

Melodic ideas are fragmentary here, but suggest the start of the second subject.

SECOND MOVEMENT: CODA – RHYTHM

Bars 163–170

Largely a phrase of flowing quavers, with the one bar of dotted rhythms that has featured throughout the movement.

Bars 170–182

The flowing quavers continue in the melody.

The texture is energised by repeated semiquavers in the violins.

Bars 182–190

Dotted rhythms are heard in the string harmony and the violin melody.

The anacrusis-to-downbeat rhythm is also heard in the oboes, and cellos and basses.

Bars 190–195

The final bars are primarily built from the anacrusis-to-downbeat pattern.

SECOND MOVEMENT: CODA – HARMONY

Bars 163–170

The harmony is constructed solely from tonic and dominant chords.

Note the V^{7}b → Ib progression at 166^3–167^1, which starts a conjunct segment in the bass line.

The violins provide an internal dominant pedal in repeated semiquavers in bars 166–170.

Bars 170–182

The previous four bars are treated to a sequence up a tone: the harmony now becomes tonic and dominant in G minor.

It seems as though another statement will follow, up a 3rd in B♭ major, but the second bar is itself treated twice to a falling sequence so that the phrase ends up back in F major.

Bars 182–190

The harmonic rhythm slows. Chords V⁷ and I alternate, each lasting for two bars.

Bars 190–195

A series of four simple perfect cadences.

The tonic chord is reiterated in the final bar.

SECOND MOVEMENT: CODA – TEXTURE

Bars 163–170

The p dynamic notwithstanding, there is a rich texture with various doublings:

- The violin melody doubled an octave lower by bassoon
- The dotted rhythm of bar 165 doubled in 3rds by second violins and bassoon
- A middle line on the horns heard in octaves
- The bass line doubled an octave higher by violas in bars 167–168.

In addition, the dotted rhythm in bar 165 is treated to a contrary-motion doubling by the oboes.

Bars 170–182

The rich texture involving virtually the full orchestra (except trumpets) continues.

Bars 182–190

The texture is still intricate, though the woodwind section is a little less full.

Bars 190–195

For a few bars a much more delicate texture, primarily in just two parts, is used before the full orchestra plays the last few chords.

SECOND MOVEMENT: CODA – INSTRUMENTATION

Bars 163–170

A skilful blend of strings and winds. Note:

- The combination of violins doubled at the lower octave by bassoon
- The rich combination of oboes and horns from bar 166³.

Bars 170–182

Woodwinds are to the fore in bars 170–174: initially clarinet and bassoon, then oboes and clarinets.

There is a full orchestral *tutti* from bar 175 except for the trumpets, who are not useful here given they are 'crooked' in C (that is, have had their length adjusted to fit the key) and we are in flat keys here – B♭ major, G minor and F major.

Bars 182–190

Highly effective scoring here:

- Each pair of wind instruments contributes at different times
- A rich string texture with double-stopped second violins and violas underpins the first violin melody.

Bars 190–195

A starring role for the horns (using notes from the harmonic series) before a full scoring of the final chords.

Writing essays

ACCESSING THE MARKS

Mark schemes for previous Unit 1 papers are available on the AQA website.

Your essays will be assessed for the following qualities:

- Knowledge and understanding of the music
- Relevance to the question set
- Points supported by references to the score
- Specialist vocabulary
- Awareness of context
- Writing style.

Bearing these factors in mind, you can see that you want to avoid the following pitfalls:

- Factual inaccuracies and inaccurate analytical comment
- Writing about aspects of the piece that are not relevant to the question
- Making general points that are not backed up by specific references to the score
- Avoiding appropriate technical terms, or using technical vocabulary in incorrect ways
- Writing with poor spelling, grammar and structure to your essay.

Writing good essays requires practice. In particular:

- The more you have studied the piece, the more your analytical understanding will be accurate and comprehensive.
- The more angles you have considered each movement from, the quicker you will locate the specific examples that will support the points you make.
- The more you use specialist vocabulary in conversation, reading about the music, making notes and writing about the piece, the more comfortable and convincing you will be in using technical terms.
- The more practice essays you write, the better your writing style will be and the more confident you will be, helping you to keep to time in the exam.

Therefore, make sure you factor into your revision schedule times when you will practise writing essays.

SAMPLE ESSAYS

Read the following essay as though you were an examiner. Consider the various factors listed above. Can you see any shortcomings? What mark out of 20 would you award this candidate?

You may like to fill in the table on the next page as you assess this answer.

Write an informative account of the introduction in the first movement of this symphony. You should refer to structure, melody, texture, instrumentation, rhythm, harmony and tonality.

Beethoven was born in Bonn in 1770 and was 30 when his first symphony was played for the first time in Vienna. The symphony is written for a large Classical orchestra with a full range of wind instruments as well as trumpets and timpani.

Following the model often used by his teacher Haydn, Beethoven starts his symphony with a slow introduction (marked Adagio molto). This begins with four homophonic bars using the whole orchestra that use a series of dominant 7th chords. The dynamics are typical of Beethoven from the outset, with *fp* markings on the downbeats. Unusually the strings are playing pizzicato.

A brief linking melody on the violins leads to the middle phrase of the introduction. Here the texture is more complicated. There is a long sustained G in the oboe and clarinet around which the harmony moves. The main melody moves stepwise in the violins doubled in octaves. Its rhythm is regular with a crotchet on the 2nd beat of the bar tied to the first of eight semiquavers in the second half of the bar. This creates a sense of forward momentum in the music, despite the slow tempo. The C#s in bar 7 mean the music has gone to D minor. A second tune of falling 3rds is played by the flutes.

A crescendo in bar 7 moves the music back to *f* for a more homophonic final phrase to the introduction. Like at the start, there is no real melody here – instead the music is made up of chords such as C major and F major in bar 8 and Ic–V in bar 9. This leads into an interrupted cadence in bar 10. The same chords are repeated in bars 10–12 mainly by the winds. Under their dominant chord in bar 12 the strings play a G major ascending scale before cancelling the F# on the way down at the end of the bar so that the music can resolve into C major and the Allegro can begin.

Beginning his symphony with this slow section makes the piece sound important and means there is a big contrast when the tempo changes for the first subject at bar 13. The violin tune here is built out of a three-note motif which is a device Beethoven often used in his melodies. The woodwind chords at bars 17–19 are similar to the chords at the start of the introduction.

Paragraph	Strengths	Weaknesses
1		
2		
3		
4		
5		

An annotated version of this answer can be found on page 84.

Here is a different answer to the same question. What is your impression of this essay?

Write an informative account of the introduction in the first movement of this symphony. You should refer to structure, melody, texture, instrumentation, rhythm, harmony and tonality.

For his first symphony Beethoven devised a very striking and attention-grabbing Adagio introduction. For this piece in C major, he starts with great originality on a C^7 chord that includes a B♭.

This initially contradictory chord is part of a very clever strategy to establish the home key of the symphony. Beethoven's plan for the introduction is to make its most important chord G, but G as a dominant and not as the tonic, so that he can resolve this onto its tonic of C major as the Allegro starts. The chord of G major is first heard at bar 4, having been approached from two degrees flatter: bar 1 is a perfect cadence of F major and bar 2 is an interrupted cadence of C major. The harmonic rhythm then halves so that bars 3–4 make up a slower and grander perfect cadence of G major. In four bars the suggestion of key centre has been pulled two degrees sharper and the expectation is that – sooner or later – the music will need to fall one step backward into C major.

The scoring of these opening homophonic bars is also very interesting. Beethoven uses a full double wind section – still quite unusual in 1800 – to sustain the chords; meanwhile, the strings give the chords more attack by playing them pizzicato.

From bar 5 there is a passage that has a building sense of anticipation. This is achieved through a harmony that is built around an inverted dominant pedal in the oboe and clarinet (decorated in various ways, such as the F♯ auxiliary notes). Several of the chords are in inversions – V^7d at bar 5^3, Ib in bar 6, Vb in bar 7 – which adds to the sense of the music searching for a strong tonic chord. The melody in the violins (in octaves) twists and turns in conjunct fashion, very slowly climbing in pitch. There is also a triadic countermelody woven into the texture on the flute and first bassoon (also the horns in bar 6) which adds to the sense of intrigue in the music.

The texture returns to being chordal at bar 8, though with antiphony between strings and winds. The Ic–V progression in bar 9 suggests that the anticipated perfect cadence in C major is due, but at the last moment the G# in the bass leads to an interrupted cadence, and we are kept waiting a little longer. The descending four-note scale in bar 9 is the first appearance of a significant motif. Another Ic–V⁷ progression at half speed (rhythmic augmentation) in bars 11–12 is scored in a manner reminiscent of bars 3–4. Under this the strings in octaves play a rising G major scale and then descend (using the four-note motif again) in C major with an F♮ to resolve onto a strong C major tonic as the Allegro begins.

This answer – only 20 per cent longer than the first one – is far superior. It shows a comprehensive understanding of the music and confines itself to answering the question. Detailed comments are given with bar (and beat) references, and there is confident use of technical vocabulary. The candidate has shown good awareness of the context, both historical and in terms of the relationship of the introduction to the whole movement. There is a mature writing style. The candidate could expect to be awarded full marks.

NOTE

Did you notice all the specialist vocabulary used here?

- Harmonic rhythm
- Homophonic
- Inverted dominant pedal
- Auxiliary note
- Conjunct
- Triadic
- Countermelody
- Antiphony
- Motif
- Rhythmic augmentation.

Are you confident in using all these terms?

Here is an answer to a different sort of question that requires you to consider a complete movement, but from one angle.

Describe the ways in which Beethoven makes use of rhythm in the second movement of this symphony.

Beethoven chooses the tempo 'Andante cantabile con moto' for the second movement of the symphony and writes the movement in ⅜ time. The key is F major. The second violins start the movement with a single melody line. There is a lilting quality to the music because it starts with an upbeat.

The same melody then enters in the violas and cellos, followed by an entry in bar 10 on bassoon and double basses, and then the first violins, flutes and oboes in bar 12. The music is like a fugue at first before settling into a more homophonic texture. The first subject ends with lots of semiquavers in the horns and a lot of sforzandos in the music, which give a jolting effect.

The second subject also starts with an upbeat and has a graceful character. After a while there is more energy in the rhythm. In bar 33 there are demisemiquavers and from bar 35 the melody has lots of semiquavers. Then there are lots of dotted rhythms from bar 42. Finally Beethoven uses triplet semiquavers as the exposition comes to an end.

The second half of the movement goes to D♭ major and again has lots of dotted rhythms. Firstly these are played by the strings and then on the timpani as the rest of the orchestra begin to concentrate on simple quavers. Beethoven provides some relaxing contrast rhythmically with two bars when the whole orchestra play dotted crotchets.

Bar 100 is the recapitulation. Here Beethoven returns to his first subject tune, but he also includes lots of semiquavers in the texture to make it sound different from the start of the movement. The second subject, however, is the same as it was before, including the triplet semiquavers. The dotted rhythms return near the end to make a more energetic passage. However, Beethoven ends the movement peacefully with the horns. The rhythm here is reduced to quavers.

How well do you think this candidate has answered the question? Does it do all the things that the examiners are looking for (as listed on page 38)?

Make a list of all the ways in which you could improve this answer. You should be producing quite a long list, because this is not a very good answer. There is some evidence that the candidate has not really been able to hear the sound of the music inside their head when looking at the score and writing their essay. What suggests this?

When you have listed all the improvements you can suggest, look at the annotated version of the essay on page 85. Were there any additional points you had overlooked? Now try to write the essay this candidate should have written.

FURTHER ESSAY TITLES

Here are some additional essay questions for you to try:

- What is the purpose of an exposition section in a symphony? Illustrate using the first movement of Beethoven's first symphony as an example.
- In the first movement of this symphony how does the recapitulation differ to the exposition?
- How does Beethoven use tonality and harmony in the development section in the first movement of this symphony?
- Describe the ways in which Beethoven builds his melodies from motifs in the first movement of the symphony.

- Write an informative account of the exposition in the second movement of this symphony. You should refer to structure, melody, texture, instrumentation, rhythm, harmony and tonality.
- How does Beethoven develop the material of the second movement of this symphony between bars 65 and 100?
- Describe the ways in which Beethoven writes for the horns, trumpets and timpani in **both** movements that you have studied in this symphony.
- Consider the coda sections of **both** movements. To what extent do these sections further develop the material used in the main parts of the movements?

Unit 1 – Section C: Historical Study – Area of Study 2 (selected topic)

The final section of the Unit 1 exam is based on your selected historical topic. You will have been learning about music from one of the following topics:

- Choral Music in the Baroque Period
- Music Theatre From 1940 to 1980
- British Popular Music From 1960 to the Present Day.

For each of these topics there will be two essay titles on the exam paper, and you only have to answer **one** question from the topic you have been studying.

In part, this is a similar challenge to the one met in Section B: a test of your ability to write well on the music you have been studying, giving good analytical detail and making use of appropriate technical vocabulary, in a way that is clearly relevant to the question you are answering.

There is, however, an extra dimension here. In Section B, where all candidates have been studying the same piece, you are allowed a copy of the score with you in the exam room. In Section C, where there are no set works and so you and your teacher have had the opportunity to select your own choice of music representative of the topic, you are not allowed to take scores into the exam. This means that Section C is also a test of your musical memory. Without the visual aid of a score to turn to, you will need to be able to recall the sound of the music in your inner ear unprompted. It is therefore very important that you factor into your revision timetable plenty of opportunity for listening to the music you have been studying in this area.

Since, across the country, a wide range of music will have been studied for these three topics, it is not possible for a book of this scope to cover every piece that you may have been looking at for your selected topic. You will need to refer to your own notes, and any textbook you have been using through the course, to remind yourself of the important facts and analysis that you have covered.

What you will find in this section is some advice for each topic on how to prepare your revision notes for this section and how to make sure you have covered a wide enough range of music for your chosen topic. There is also some advice on essay writing, and a sample essay for you to assess as though you were an examiner.

The marking of Section C essays is very similar to Section B. Examiners will be looking for the following strengths in your essay:

- Sound knowledge and understanding of the music
- Clear relevance to the question set
- Specific points supported by references to the score
- Correct and confident use of specialist vocabulary
- An awareness of context
- A mature writing style.

If you have been working on music theatre, turn to page 48. If you have chosen British popular music, turn to page 52. The section on Baroque choral music follows on straightaway. Annotated versions of the sample answers to these questions can be found on pages 87–93.

Area of Study 2a: Choral Music in the Baroque Period

ORGANISING YOUR REVISION NOTES

You need to be prepared for questions that can come from three angles:

- Types of movement: choruses, arias, recitatives

  Example: Choose two contrasting arias from the music you have studied, and write informatively about each.

- Different moods of music, as suggested by the lyrics and realised in the music

  *Example: How did Baroque composers convey a mood of majesty in their choral music? Refer to **at least two** different pieces of music in your answer.*

- Different composers

  *Example: Contrast music by **two** different composers of the Baroque period, highlighting aspects of their choral writing.*

In each case the question may steer you to talk about one or two elements of music only, such as melody, harmony and tonality, rhythm, texture, or use of voices.

*Example: Choose **two** contrasting movements by the **same** composer and write about the way harmony and texture are used.*

Bearing all these aspects in mind, it would be a good idea to organise your revision notes for this section in a methodical manner so that you have a systematic approach to learning information about different pieces that might combine to answer one of these questions.

Use a separate piece of paper for each movement you have studied, and organise it in a way that will allow you to separate out all the different elements. For example:

TITLE OF MOVEMENT
Composer:
Chorus / Aria / Recitative:
Mood:
Structure
Melody
Harmony / tonality
Rhythm
Texture
Timbre / use of voices

With the information organised this way, when you are writing a practice essay you can have the relevant pages to hand that suit just that essay, and – if the question specifies only certain elements of music – refer to those sections of each page of your revision notes.

SAMPLE ESSAY

Read the following essay as though you were an examiner. Consider the various factors listed on pages 44–45. Can you see any shortcomings? What mark out of 20 would you award this candidate?

Choose two contrasting arias from the music you have studied, and write informatively about each.

I am going to write about two arias from Handel's oratorio Messiah, which he wrote in 1741 for a performance in Dublin. The two arias I have chosen are 'The trumpet shall sound' and 'He was despised'.

'The trumpet shall sound' comes in part 3 of the oratorio, and is probably Handel's best-known aria for the bass voice. There is also a very important trumpet part, as suggested to Handel by the text.

There is a long introduction in which the main theme is presented on the trumpet, an immediate response to the text of the previous recitative. There are a few instances of dialogue between the trumpet and the strings. Cadences are decorated by trills in the trumpet, which gives a virtuoso touch. The bass soloist enters in bar 28. His melody is similar to the trumpet tune, and has a rising scale for 'dead shall be raised'. The very long 'A' section has a short interlude in the middle for the trumpet to give the singer a rest. It ends with a dramatic interrupted cadence and a final bar for the singer alone. The trumpet again stars in the postlude.

In the middle section, it is the trumpeter who has a rest, as the singer takes over. This middle section makes a contrast, being in B minor and having a more lyrical mood. The whole of the first section is then played again, to finish the aria in a blaze of trumpet sound.

'He was despised' is an alto aria in da capo form, with a strong contrast of mood midway. It begins in a warm E♭ major in a broad *Largo* tempo. There is a rich string tone in the first bar, but as early as bar 2 a falling three-note pattern in 3rds, suggestive of falling tears, captures a sense of sorrow. This is reinforced before the introduction is finished by some rich harmony that briefly visits a mournful E♭ minor and has several aching suspensions.

In the 'A' section the soloist's vocal line has many expressive features such as appoggiaturas on 'despised and rejected', several falling scales such as the one on 'sorrows', and the violin melody from the E♭ minor segment of the introduction for the words 'and acquainted with grief'. Perhaps most telling, as the 'A' section comes to a close, is the unaccompanied singing on 'he was despised, rejected' that conveys loneliness, and is punctuated by the tear motif. This is followed by the emotionally charged diminished 7th chord in the orchestra on 'man of sorrow', which is sustained for a bar and a half:

In the middle section, Handel portrays the scourging of Christ on Good Friday through a succession of relentless dotted rhythms in the strings. At the start of this section the key has changed to a dark C minor, and it gradually changes to G minor as the music becomes more intense. The harmony through this section is very expressive, with a number of suspensions and a powerful circle of 5ths progression midway through.

> The middle section ends dramatically: the orchestra's whipping dotted rhythms suddenly break off, and the alto soloist sings 'from shame and spitting' unaccompanied and in declamatory syllabic style that almost literally spits out the words. A simple but forthright perfect cadence ends the passage before the da capo returns the mood to the aching music of the opening section.

How well do you think the candidate has done? What are the strengths and weaknesses of the essay? Are both arias equally well treated? Has the candidate been able to 'hear' the music for both arias in the silence of the exam room? Refer to the annotated version on pages 87–89 to see how an examiner might have viewed the essay. You will find there some valuable advice for this candidate that might help you in the exam room.

FURTHER ESSAY TITLES

Here are some additional essay questions on this topic for you to try:

- What is a recitative? Explain by referring to **two** passages of recitative that you have studied, and highlight ways in which the music is expressive of the words.
- How did Baroque composers create a mood of **either** celebration **or** sadness in their music? Refer to music by **at least two** composers in your answer.
- Describe the ways in which Baroque composers have used **melody** and **texture** in their music. Refer to **at least two** pieces of music in your answer.

Area of Study 2b: Music Theatre: a study of the musical from 1940 to 1980

ORGANISING YOUR REVISION NOTES

You need to be prepared for questions that can come from three angles:

- Types of number: solo songs, ensembles, music for the chorus, music for dance

  Example: Choose two contrasting solo songs from the music you have studied, and write informatively about each.

- Different moods of music, as suggested by the lyrics or characters in the story and realised in the music

  Example: Write an essay describing how composers have used music to help to portray different characters. Refer to suitable passages from the musicals that you have studied.

- Different composers

  Example: Choose one of the following composers and write an essay that assesses his significance in the history of the musical between 1940 and 1980:

  Bernstein; Lloyd Webber; Loewe; Rodgers; Sondheim

In each case the question may steer you to talk about one or two elements of music only, such as melody, harmony and tonality, rhythm, texture, or use of voices.

*Example: Choose **two** contrasting passages from **one** musical you have studied and show how the composer has used melody and rhythm to enhance the drama.*

Bearing all these aspects in mind, you will find it helpful to organise your revision notes for this section in a methodical manner that allows for a systematic approach to learning information about different pieces that might combine to answer one of these questions.

Use a separate piece of paper for each number you have studied, and organise it in a way that will allow you to separate out all the different elements. For example:

TITLE OF NUMBER AND SHOW
Composer: Solo / Ensemble / Chorus / Dance: Mood:
Structure
Melody
Harmony / tonality
Rhythm
Texture
Timbre / use of voices

With the information organised this way, when you are writing a practice essay you can have the relevant pages to hand that suit just that essay, and – if the question specifies only certain elements of music – refer to those sections of each page of your revision notes.

SAMPLE ESSAY

Read the following essay as though you were an examiner. Consider the various factors listed on pages 44–45. Can you see any shortcomings? What mark out of 20 would you award this candidate?

Choose two contrasting solo songs from the music you have studied, and write informatively about each.

I am going to write about 'I could have danced all night' from *My Fair Lady* by Frederick Loewe, and 'Take back your mink' from *Guys and Dolls* by Frank Loesser.

My Fair Lady was a big hit on Broadway in 1956, and is adapted from George Bernard Shaw's play *Pygmalion*. The story is concerned with issues of class: Eliza, a cockney flower-girl, is trained by Professor Higgins to speak like an aristocratic girl, all because of a bet he makes with a friend (Colonel Pickering). The song comes when Eliza, at the end of a long day, finally starts to speak with the proper posh accent.

Mrs Pearce tells everyone to go to bed, and the music immediately starts up with an introductory section. The music is energetic and happy, with chirping woodwind chords. The vocal line ('Bed, bed, I couldn't go to bed') is similarly lively, with a fast tempo and short phrases.

The introduction is brief, and soon the main melody is heard. Here the vocal line is rather different: long phrases that include long notes (on 'danced', 'night' and 'more' in the opening phrase, for example) and this makes for a melody that expresses the dreamy mood that Eliza is now in. However, the chirpy and bubbly mood of the introduction is also present in the way the woodwinds accompany the singer with rapid quavers. This makes for a skilful musical portrayal of Eliza's feelings and accounts for the song's popularity. To further intensify the impact of the song, the final phrase ('I only know...') starts with a dramatic hold-back.

The main melody is repeated for a second verse, which includes some counterpoint from the maids trying to help Eliza get to bed. A third verse starts softly, but builds to a big climax, with Eliza finishing on a long sustained top G – an ending sure to inspire applause from the audience.

In 'Take back your mink' there is a slightly longer introduction. The rhythm is free – almost recitative-style – with a sense of natural speech, and pauses between each phrase. The melodic contour twists and turns in conjunct fashion, adding to the conversational flavour. Harmonically, the passage avoids any strong use of the tonic chord, which creates a sense of anticipation (where it is used, a flattened 7th is quickly introduced to move forwards to chord IV). The introduction ends with a prolonged dominant 7th.

The main refrain takes the character of an elegant Viennese waltz – conveying the sophistication of the lyrics (mink, pearls, etc.) and the romanticism of young lovers. The melodic idea is a simple two-bar shape, which is treated to a falling sequence:

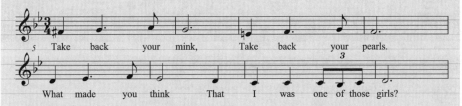

Take back your mink, Take back your pearls.

What made you think That I was one of those girls?

The refrain follows the standard AABA song form, and the second line follows a very similar phrase, slightly adjusted at the end. For the third line, however, Loesser changes the metre to $\frac{2}{3}$. This, coupled with a simple vocal line alternating between two notes, shows that the elegance of the waltz was just Adelaide maintaining dignity: now we realise she is in a strop! The waltz metre returns for the final 'A' phrase, and a confident perfect cadence that – finally – conclusively finds the tonic chord.

The scoring of the song is for a dance band: trumpets and saxes to the fore, and some rich bass clarinet on the bass line. There is a very telling short trumpet solo in the opening section at 'one night in his apartment' which calls for the wah-wah mute that gives a suggestive tone.

After Adelaide has sung the refrain, her 'dolls' repeat it in an upbeat $\frac{4}{4}$ version that makes the mood more defiant. A further version for dancing is played as an instrumental.

How well do you think the candidate has done? What are the strengths and weaknesses of the essay? Are both songs equally well treated? Has the candidate been able to 'hear' the music for both songs in the silence of the exam room? Refer to the annotated version on pages 89–91 to see how an examiner might have viewed the essay. You will find there some valuable advice for this candidate that might help you in the exam room.

FURTHER ESSAY TITLES

Here are some additional essay questions on this topic for you to try:

- Compare **two** passages of music from different musicals that you have studied that are intended for dance, and highlight the musical features that make them effective.
- Choose a character from any musical you have studied, and discuss how the musical features of the songs for that character create a portrayal of their personality.
- How are melody and texture used in the writing for chorus in music theatre? Refer to **at least two** different shows.

Area of Study 2c: British Popular Music from 1960 to the Present Day

ORGANISING YOUR REVISION NOTES

You need to be prepared for questions that can come from three angles:

- Historical, by decade

  Example: Choose two songs written in the 1970s, and write in detail about the musical content of each song.

- Different moods of music, as suggested by the lyrics or message of the song and realised in the music

  Example: Popular music has become increasingly used for social comment during this period. Choose two contrasting songs and write in detail about how the music is used to reflect the meaning of the words.

- By different artist or band

  Example: Choose one of the following bands and write an essay that assesses their significance in the history of British popular music since 1960:

  The Beatles; Coldplay; Duran Duran; Oasis; Pink Floyd.

In each case the question may steer you to talk about one or two elements of music only, such as melody, harmony and tonality, rhythm, texture, or the use of voices.

*Example: Choose **two** songs of contrasting mood from the 1980s and show how the artist or band has used melody and structure in their song.*

Bearing all these aspects in mind, you will find it helpful to organise your revision notes for this section in a methodical manner that allows for a systematic approach to learning information about different pieces that might combine to answer one of these questions.

Use a separate piece of paper for each song you have studied, and organise it in a way that will allow you to separate out all the different elements. For example:

TITLE OF SONG
Band / Artist: **Decade:**   **Mood:**
Structure
Melody

Harmony / tonality	
Rhythm	
Texture	
Timbre / use of voices	

With the information organised this way, when you are writing a practice essay you can have the relevant pages to hand that suit just that essay, and – if the question specifies only certain elements of music – refer to those sections of each page of your revision notes.

SAMPLE ESSAY

Read the following essay as though you were an examiner. Consider the various factors listed on pages 44–45. Can you see any shortcomings? What mark out of 20 would you award this candidate?

Choose two songs written in the 1970s, and write in detail about the musical content of each song.

I am going to write about two great songs from the 70s: 'Speak To Me – Breathe' from Pink Floyd's iconic album *The Dark Side of the Moon*, and 'Somebody To Love' by the famous rock band Queen.

Pink Floyd were a London-based band who came to fame in the late 60s with their elaborate light shows. When the line-up changed in 1968, their music changed direction, and became focused on various forms of alienation such as madness and death, which appealed to those growing up in the shadow of Vietnam and the Cold War. *The Dark Side of the Moon* was released in 1973 and is the fifth highest-selling album of all time. 'Speak To Me – Breathe' is the first song on the album.

'Speak To Me' is largely not traditional music but a collage of sound effects starting with a heartbeat, created through a dampened bass drum. Other sounds heard include ticking clocks, manic laughter, a cash register and a helicopter, all sounds which were to reappear in other songs in the album. There are also fragments of conversation about madness layered on top. At the end a reversed piano chord completes the sense of build-up as the track leads immediately on into 'Breathe'.

'Breathe' has a more clearly defined beat at a slow tempo (typical of Pink Floyd) in four-time. The bass drum gives a strong downbeat to the rhythm. There is a more distinct verse structure here: eight lines that come in two halves – a change of chord sequence marking the halfway point. The same music provides an instrumental introduction with guitars and frequent slow pitch-bending. The song links into the next track on the album, 'On The Run'.

As prosperity grew in the 1970s, pop concerts increasingly were held at large stadiums such as Wembley. The song by Queen 'Somebody To Love' is representative of a style that suits such events, a style now called 'stadium rock'. The song is influenced by gospel music, especially of the style sung by Aretha Franklin. Using the latest in 1970s technology, the band members multi-tracked their voices to create the aural illusion of a 100-strong gospel choir.

The introduction to the song is sung with discreet piano backing and has a free approach to rhythm, with frequent pauses, that is typical of gospel music. The voices start on A♭ and fan out in contrary motion in a homophonic choral style.

When the first verse starts the music goes into a strict tempo (a compound four in a bar) and there is a confident, marching quality, heightened by the harmony that concentrates on major chords and keeps moving towards the sharper dominant key. This is achieved by using a B♭ major chord when the song is in A♭ major. Freddie Mercury sings the melody whilst other members of the band provide the backing vocals in a multi-tracked gospel style. The main melody tends to have a rising contour that allows for some impassioned singing at the top of the male range. Falsetto is also used at times. The 'somebody to love' line provides an infectious melodic hook, and the drumming (by Roger Taylor) makes heavy use of the crash cymbal.

There are two verses, and then a short middle section which provides a balance to the harmony of the verse by visiting the flat side: D♭ major , G♭ major, and G♭ minor. This then passes into an instrumental solo for the lead guitar (played by Brian May), which is based on the chord sequence of the verse. Voices join in at the end and lead into another vocal verse. This, however, breaks off before the refrain, and the line 'need somebody to love' is repeated many times, building from an a cappella start. A final refrain follows.

There is then a coda with several more repetitions of 'find me somebody to love', with rhythmic hand-clapping providing an infectious feature for audience participation: a significant element of stadium rock.

How well do you think the candidate has done? What are the strengths and weaknesses of the essay? Are both songs equally well treated? Has the candidate been able to 'hear' the music for both songs in the silence of the exam room? Refer to the annotated version on pages 91–93 to see how an examiner might have viewed the essay. You will find there some valuable advice for this candidate that might help you in the exam room.

FURTHER ESSAY TITLES

Here are some additional essay questions on this topic for you to try:

- What are the main differences in musical style between songs of the decade 1980–1990 and songs from the years 2000–2010? Refer to at least two songs from each period.
- What musical features make the difference between a typical ballad and a protest song?
- Choose **one** artist working in British popular music during the period, and highlight features typical of their style.

Unit 2 – Creating Musical Ideas

Content

For Unit 2 you have to write music to one of three briefs:

- Brief A: Compositional techniques
- Brief B: Free composition or pastiche in response to a given genre
- Brief C: Arranging.

Details about what exactly is required in each year are produced on the Creating Musical Ideas paper, which is available from 1 November. Your teacher will make this available to you at the point they think best fits into the course schedule that they have devised. In all, you have 20 hours of **controlled time** in which to complete one of the three briefs. Your work has to be submitted by 15 May (so you may be starting on your submission as late as April), and needs to comprise:

- A score or annotation of the music you have composed
- A recording of the piece(s) you are submitting
- The Candidate Record Form, which you must sign.

The score or annotation can be written by hand or printed from a computer. If you are answering Brief A you may write your answer on the actual question paper (but do not have to do it this way). Note that Brief A comprises two questions.

The recording may be an acoustic one of musicians performing your music, or one of the computer playback; it is an important aid to the examiner and not part of the actual assessment. The recording may be made after the 20 hours of controlled time have passed.

As this unit is more like coursework than an exam, there is no real revision required and it lies outside the main focus of this book. However, for each brief, there follows a checklist that you might use as you are getting ready to finish your work and prepare it for submission to the examiners.

> **NOTE**
>
> Note that you will not be allowed to take this book into the room where you are completing your Unit 2 work under controlled time, but you can refer to it between sessions and remind yourself of important aspects that you wish to check just before you start a controlled-time session.

Brief A – question 1

Checklist:

- Do you know what key the melody is in?
- Have you found all the modulations to related keys that occur during the melody?
- Have you finished each phrase with a suitable cadence in the right place?
- Have you used a mix of root position and first-inversion chords?
- Are all diminished chords (VII in major keys, II and VII in minor keys) in first inversion?
- Are second inversions only used in correct passing and cadential patterns?
- Have you put in all necessary accidentals when the music modulates?
- Whenever you have V^7, does the dominant 7th note fall by step on the next beat?
- Does each voice part sit in an appropriate register?
- Are the A, T and B parts easy to sing, avoiding intervals such as the augmented 4th?
- Have you found opportunity for some passing notes in lower parts?
- Do your passing notes always move by step?
- Have you checked every pair of parts to make sure there are no parallel 5ths or octaves? (Check: S/A, S/T, S/B, A/T, A/B, T/B.)

Brief A – question 2

Checklist:

- Have you chosen an appropriate tempo for your piece and provided the relevant marking at the top of the score?
- Have you indicated what instruments you are using?
- Does each melody have an essentially consonant fit with the given part, with any dissonant notes justified as passing notes, auxiliary notes or suspensions?
- Do your two melodic lines complement each other well, giving each other space in which to be heard?
- Have you made good use of the potential register for each of your chosen melodic instruments?
- Is the bass line of the given material always at the bottom of the texture throughout the piece?
- Is there a good rhythmic character to your piece?
- Do your melodic lines have a variety of conjunct and disjunct motion?
- Is there a sense of phrase structure to your melodies?
- Have you spotted and utilised any sequential passages in the given accompaniment?
- Is there a variety of textures in your piece?
- Have you made sure there are no parallel 5ths or octaves between the two melodic lines **and** between each melody and the given bass part?
- Are the melodic lines edited with appropriate phrasing, bowing, articulation and dynamic markings?

Brief B

Checklist:

- Does your piece have a clear and effective structure?
- Is there some contrast of tonality?
- Is there a good rhythmic character to your piece?
- Are the melodic ideas well shaped and memorable?
- Have you developed the melodic material and not relied solely on simple repetition?
- If your piece includes singing, does the text fit the melodic line convincingly?
- Have you created interest in your harmonic writing (for example: primary *and* secondary chords, different inversions, chromatic inflections, modulation, changing harmonic rhythm, pedal notes)?
- Is there something imaginative and varied in your handling of texture?
- Have you explored the full range of your chosen instruments in your use of register?
- Have you considered the changes of timbre that your chosen instruments offer?
- *Either:* is your score well edited with clear performance directions regarding tempo, dynamics and phrasing; *or:* does your annotation set out clearly the structure and musical content of your piece in a way that will communicate your creative ideas directly to the examiner?

Brief C

Checklist:

- Does your piece have a clear and effective structure?
- Is the majority of your piece clearly based on the given melody?
- Have you found some variety to the way you have handled the melody: for example a change of metre, a change of tonality, or a decorated version of the melody?
- Does the accompaniment to the melody have a distinct rhythmic identity?
- Have you found ways of giving the harmonic content of the arrangement interest?
- Is there something imaginative in your handling of the texture?
- Does the melody appear in a variety of registers?
- Are there ways in which your arrangement reflects the words of the folk song?
- Have you considered the changes of timbre that your chosen instruments offer?
- *Either:* is your score well edited with clear performance directions regarding tempo, dynamics and phrasing; *or:* does your annotation set out clearly the structure and musical content of your piece in a way that will communicate your creative ideas directly to the examiner?

Unit 3 – Interpreting Musical Ideas

Content

For Unit 3 you have to offer **two** of the following six options:

1. A solo performance on an instrument
2. A solo performance on voice
3. A solo performance on a second instrument
4. An ensemble performance
5. Technology option 1: sequencing
6. Technology option 2: multi-track or close-microphone recording.

Details of what is involved for each option are available in the AQA specification. You can complete your chosen two options at any point during the AS course. Your work needs to be submitted to an AQA moderator by 15 May, but needs to be marked by your teacher first, so they will give you an earlier deadline. Your submission will need to comprise:

- The recording relevant to each of your two chosen options
- Supporting material such as scores for your performances, original material for the piece you chose to sequence in option 5, and/or the initial capture of the recording you have made for option 6
- The Candidate Record Form, which you must sign, and on which your teacher will write their marks and supporting comments.

As this unit is more like coursework than an exam, there is no real revision required and it lies outside the main focus of this book. However, some checklists are provided below that you might use as you are getting ready to complete your work for this unit, so that your submission makes a favourable impression on the moderator.

Solo performances (options 1–3)

Checklist:

- Is your programme 5–8 minutes in duration?
- Is that 5–8 minutes of you playing and not relying on long introductions?
- Is that 5–8 minutes without relying on repeats of the same music played the same way?
- Are you playing the music accurately?

- Are you performing the music at the correct tempo?
- Have you given each piece a well-shaped interpretation with a good dynamic range, consideration of articulation, and appropriate use of rubato or tempo changes?
- Are you confident in the manner in which you are performing the music?
- Have you listened to the recording? If you can perform the music more accurately, or with a stronger sense of interpretation or communication, it will pay to do another take (though this will depend on how hard you have practised).
- Is the quality of the recording good?

Ensemble performance (option 4)

All the points in the checklist for solo performance apply here too. In addition:

- Does your choice of music require an ensemble of **at least three** musicians? (If your choice is only a duet, you should take advice on whether the music suits an ensemble option.)
- Is your part a unique line in the texture (i.e. not doubled by another musician)?
- Is there a tight sense of ensemble (rhythmic co-ordination) in the performance – especially at any points that the tempo changes?
- Is there a good balance of dynamic between all the musicians in the ensemble?

Sequencing (option 5)

Checklist:

- Is the original piece you have chosen to sequence **at least 32** bars long?
- Are there **at least four** independent instrumental or voice parts?
- Have you checked that a score of the original piece is being submitted with your work?
- Is one of the parts a recording of a live (acoustic) performance?
- Have you checked your sequenced version of the piece against the score for accuracy of pitch and rhythm?
- Have you made appropriate use of timbres and techniques such as panning?
- Have you considered details such as dynamics and articulation in your sequenced version?
- Does your version capture a sense of the style of the piece?
- Have you given details of the equipment you have used for your work, and the processes and decisions involved with producing your final version?

Multi-track or close-microphone recording (option 6)

Checklist:

- Is the original piece you have chosen to record **at least 32** bars long?
- Are there **at least four** independent instrumental or voice parts?
- Have you checked that a score of the original piece is being submitted with your work?
- Is the initial capture that you made of the recording included in the submission?
- Does your edited recording have a good balance and dynamic range?
- Have you made effective musical use of techniques such as reverb and delay?
- Is the quality of the recording good across a wide range of frequencies?
- Have you given details of the equipment you have used for your work, and the processes and decisions involved with producing your final edited recording?

Answers and comments on exercises for Unit 1 – Section A: Listening

EXERCISE 1

The music for the rhythm you have heard is:

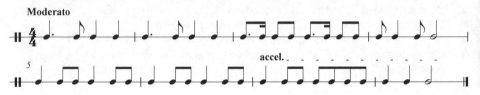

ANSWERS

a. $\frac{4}{4}$
b. 8
c. Bars 1 and 2 (or bars 5 and 6)
d. Bar 3 is the rhythmic diminution of bars 1 and 2 (every note value is halved)
e. Syncopation
f. Accelerando.

COMMENTS

■ The rhythm has a march-like character, typical of music in $\frac{4}{4}$ at a moderate tempo.
■ Count the bars by thinking: **1**–2–3–4; **2**–2–3–4; **3**–2–3–4; **4** …
■ The syncopation in bar 4 is because a half-beat is emphasised. It cannot be a hemiola, because the music is not in triple time ($\frac{3}{2}$).
■ You should be able to hear the pulse getting faster towards the end.

EXERCISE 2

The music for the rhythm you have heard is:

ANSWERS

a. $\frac{3}{4}$
b. 9
c. Third
d. Dotted rhythm

e. Triplet rhythm
f. Hemiola.

COMMENTS

■ The rhythm has a gentle lilting quality that is common of music in triple time.

■ Count the bars carefully! There is one more than you might reasonably guess...

■ Careful listening is required to hear that the music starts with an upbeat. It is difficult to realise on first listening, but as the opening becomes more familiar on subsequent hearings, it should be clear that the second beat you hear is more stressed than the first.

■ The hemiola should be clear to hear. From bar 5 try counting like this:
1–2–3; **1**–2–3; **1**–and–2–and–3–and; **1**.

■ There is a very distinctive kick in the rhythm that is only possible in triple time.

EXERCISE 3

The music for the rhythm you have heard is:

ANSWERS

a. ⁶⁄₈
b. 2
c. 1
d. Quaver
e. Bar 7
f. Ritenuto.

COMMENTS

■ You should feel quite clearly that there are only two beats in each bar. If in doubt, think like a soldier marching: 'left, right, left, right'.

■ However, each beat subdivides into three, which makes for a compound time signature. Think: **I**–and–a–2–and–a; **1**–and–a–2–and–a; **1** ...

■ This means that the 'beat' is a dotted crotchet, so that the subdivision can be represented by three quavers (which, of course, makes one-and-a-half crotchets).

■ Therefore the first – unaccented – note at the start is just a quaver.

- You should be able to hear the pulse getting slower towards the end.

EXERCISE 4

The music for the rhythm you have heard is:

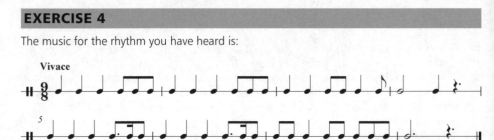

ANSWERS

a. Additive
b. 4
c. It is longer than beats 1, 2 and 3 (being worth a dotted crotchet)
d. 8
e. The 4th beat now has a dotted rhythm pattern.

COMMENTS

- The slightly lopsided 'limp' to the rhythm here is due to the additive rhythm.
- The four beats per bar are three crotchets and one dotted crotchet.

EXERCISE 5

The music for the melody you have heard is:

ANSWERS

a. Major
b. Conjunct and diatonic
c. Conjunct
d. Triadic
e. It is chromatic
f. Bars 1–4: both phrases are conjunct

g. A turn at the end of bars 2 and 6.

COMMENTS

■ The melody has that bright, sunny mood of a major key which is evident from the third note.

■ The music in bars 1–4 is diatonic because there are no sharps or flats; there are no leaps in contour, so the melody is conjunct; scalic is not so appropriate since it twists and changes direction several times (unlike a scale).

■ In bars 5–6 none of the notes are neighbours, so you might think disjunct was a good description; however, all the notes here (Cs, Es and Gs) belong to a tonic chord of C major, so triadic is a much more precise description.

■ The sharps and flats in bars 7–8 make the music chromatic (rather than diatonic), but there are no leaps here, so it is once again conjunct.

EXERCISE 6

The music for the melody you have heard is:

ANSWERS

a. Minor
b. Scalic
c. Bars 1 and 2: descending; bars 3 and 4: ascending; bars 5 and 6: descending
d. It becomes disjunct
e. A trill
f. An octave.

COMMENTS

■ The melody hints at a minor key almost immediately due to the fall of a tone from the first note (which is, as in many tunes, the tonic). Were it in a major key, the leading note would be a semitone below the tonic. The G♯ in bar 3 confirms the key.

■ The falling scales in bars 1 and 2 take the form of descending melodic minor scales (with F♮ and G♮).

■ The rising scales in bars 3 and 4 follow an ascending melodic scale (with F♯ and G♯).

■ Bars 7 and 8 comprise a series of wide leaps, creating a distinctly disjunct outline.

EXERCISE 7

The music for the melody you have heard is:

ANSWERS

a. 6
b. It is a sequence of the first phrase, at a lower pitch
c. It is the inversion of the first half of the melody
d. A pentatonic scale.

COMMENTS

- The melody is clearly structured with six two-bar phrases.
- You need to listen carefully to hear the inversion in the second half of the melody.
- The pentatonic character is audible with a mix of tones and minor 3rds in the melodic line.

EXERCISE 8

The music for the melody you have heard is:

ANSWERS

a. Use of blue notes; syncopation
b. A glissando
c. It becomes scalic; it uses a whole-tone scale; it is played staccato
d. Pizzicato.

COMMENTS

■ The melody is, essentially, in a major key: as confirmed by the E♮ in bar 2. but the E♭s in bar 1 immediately give a 'blues' sound. The G♭ and E♭ in bar 3, and B♭ at the end are also 'blue notes'.

■ The glissando in bar 4 is played on the violin by sliding a finger down the string whilst bowing.

■ The whole-tone scale makes for a very haunting effect; every interval is a tone.

EXERCISE 9

Here are the eight different versions of the missing bar 3:

COMMENTS

In (a) you should have heard that the first missing note is the same as the last given note. The melody then falls stepwise and the link to the final note is the standard leading note-to-tonic semitone step.

In versions (b) to (d) you can hear that the first missing note is a step down from the last given note. Each then has its own contour. In (b) you should hear that the last missing note is the same as the note in bar 4. In (c) listen carefully for the last missing note: it is just a step above the tonic in bar 4, and this creates a small jump (of a 3rd) in the contour of bar 3. In (d) there is a leap either side of the last note in bar 3, and it is important to realise that the melody ends dominant to tonic: a sound that you should be able to recognise confidently (think of the first two notes of 'O Little Town of Bethlehem', or the opening notes of Mozart's *Eine kleine Nachtmusik*).

There is a catch in (e): the first missing note is lower than the last given note, but not by step. Instead it starts on the tonic – a note you have heard three times in the first six notes of the melody. The contour of the missing bar here is all conjunct.

In versions (f) to (h) the first missing note is a step up from the last given note. There are some leaps to work out in these versions, which makes it important to think about the link to the note in bar 4. In (f) and (h) this is the standard leading note-to-tonic semitone, but in (g) it is a falling octave – an interval that is fairly clear to hear. The E♭ in (h) is a tricky note to identify: you should be able to hear that it is higher than the previous note, but it has a distinct colour (almost a 'blue' note). Remember 'chromatic' means 'colour': the E♭ makes it distinctly different to the version in (f).

EXERCISE 10

Here is the music you have just heard:

ANSWERS

a. Major
b. An upper auxiliary note
c. An imperfect cadence
d. A passing note
e. A perfect cadence: Ic–V–I
f. No. It ends in the dominant.

COMMENTS

- The music has a confident, bright character, and is clearly in a major key.
- Both decorative notes are in the melody and should be clear to hear at the slow tempo.
- The first cadence ends on a different chord from the opening tonic chord; however, the music is not left hanging in mid-air as with an interrupted cadence. It is therefore an imperfect cadence. This one is Ic–V, otherwise known as a half-close.

- The final cadence is much more commanding and clearly a perfect cadence. The same note is in the bass for both chords that precede the final tonic chord: a common occurrence and a certain clue to a Ic–V–I cadence.
- If you don't spot it on first listening, you can hear when the second playing starts that the music ended in a different key from where it began. The move to the dominant is achieved through an extra sharp (in this case C♯), which makes the music sound brighter when it first appears.

EXERCISE 11

Here is the music you have just heard:

ANSWERS

a. Minor
b. A pedal note
c. Second time it is a dominant pedal; at the start it was a tonic pedal
d. Yes
e. A plagal cadence (IV–I)
f. A tierce de Picardie.

COMMENTS

- From the very start the music has the dark character of a minor key.
- The pedal notes are reiterated in between each chord to make them clearer to hear.
- You should be able to hear the same tonic chord starting the second listening as was present at the end of the first hearing.
- The tonic note is present in the penultimate chord as well as the final chord: a good way to test for a plagal cadence. (In a perfect cadence the leading note is in the penultimate chord, and the tonic would clash with this if you try singing it at the same time.)
- Although the tonic is the same at the end as at the beginning, the final chord has a bright major third: the hallmark of a tierce de Picardie.

EXERCISE 12

Here is the music you have just heard:

ANSWERS

a. Dissonant
b. A circle of 5ths progression
c. An interrupted cadence (Ic–V–VI)
d. A minor: the relative minor
e. A perfect cadence (Ic–V⁷–I).

COMMENTS

- The first chord is an abrasive, clashing combination of notes and not related to the key suggested by the opening arpeggio. It is therefore dissonant.
- Listen carefully for the note in the bass on the downbeat of each bar to hear the circle of 5ths. This always produces a descending sequence in the harmony. Sometimes, though not on this occasion, the melody will follow suit and also have a sequence when the circle of 5ths is used in the harmony.
- Despite the silence, the cadence at the end of the flowing melody leaves an open-ended feel, and one senses more music is needed: a sure sign of an interrupted cadence.
- The rather surprise ending takes the music to the relative minor. Try playing the piece with the following three bars instead to stay in C major:

EXERCISE 13

Here is the music you have just heard:

ANSWERS

a. Modal
b. It is an appoggiatura
c. The harmonic rhythm is much faster (every beat rather than one chord per bar)
d. There is a suspension.

COMMENTS

■ The piece has a sense of a minor mood, but the leading note is never sharpened, and this means that chord V is never heard as a major triad (e.g. bars 4 and 8). The result means that the piece has the plaintive feel of music in a minor mode (in this case the Aeolian mode).

- There is a blatant clash on the first downbeat between the note in the melody and the note in the bass. The chord fills in and the melody resolves to a harmony note. Given that the melody note on the downbeat was approached by leap from the anacrusis, this makes it an appoggiatura. Several others can be heard in the piece.
- Contrast in music can be provided in many ways; here the middle phrase gains much of its different character from the quicker harmonic rhythm, one of the more subtle but telling ways of achieving contrast.
- The suspension on the last chord is found in the middle of the chord; the D from the previous chord is reiterated as the 4th in the tonic chord and finally resolves to the 3rd.

EXERCISE 14

Here is the music you have just heard:

ANSWERS AND COMMENTS ON EXERCISES FOR UNIT 1 – SECTION A: LISTENING

ANSWERS

a. Melody with accompaniment
b. The melody is heard in the bass (or left hand of the piano)
c. Major 6th
d. A turn
e. Interrupted cadence
f. Plagal cadence.

COMMENTS

- There is a clear, single melodic line which is accompanied by a chordal figuration (known as an Alberti bass).
- For the second phrase the texture inverts: the melody is played in a lower register.
- The upbeat is the dominant note, but this rises to the third and not the tonic (in much the same way that 'My Bonnie Lies Over the Ocean' starts).
- The piece could end after the third phrase if the Ic–V progression in bar 11 resolved onto chord I for a perfect cadence in bar 12, but this is sidestepped to make an interrupted cadence.
- The penultimate chord has the tonic in the melody – a strong clue to this being a plagal ending.

EXERCISE 15

Here is the music you have just heard:

ANSWERS

a. Contrapuntal
b. Minor
c. The opening music returns but the texture is inverted – that is, the original upper melody is now in the bass
d. Perfect cadence
e. Trill
f. Inverted mordent.

COMMENTS

■ There are two strands to the texture, and both have a strong melodic character with independent rhythms and contours. This makes the music strongly contrapuntal.

■ The minor flavour is apparent from the very beginning: there is a minor 3rd on the downbeat and immediately the tonic in the bass is decorated with the sharpened leading note.

■ Fix the opening to the upper line in your memory – an A minor broken chord in crotchets, and listen for this shape in the bass when the music turns f. Meanwhile, what was the bass at the start – a conjunct shape built from a rising A minor scale – is now in the upper line at this point.

EXERCISE 16

Here is the music you have just heard:

ANSWERS

a. Canonic
b. Major
c. C major
d. $\frac{3}{4}$
e. Hemiola
f. Perfect cadence.

COMMENTS

- Throughout the piece the bass line copies the melody, starting one bar later and one octave lower.
- The melody is largely conjunct and, but for a few accidentals, outlines an F major scale fairly clearly.
- The appearance of B♮s from bar 12 makes the music sound brighter and lifts the piece into its dominant key of C major.
- The music has the lilting feel of triple time, though at this speed you might count one in a bar.
- The hemiola is a little hidden, but the combined accentuation between the two hands highlights, from bar 12: **1**–2–3; **1**–2–3; **1**–and–2–and–3–and; **1**.

EXERCISE 17

Here is the music you have just heard:

ANSWERS

a. Homophonic
b. $\frac{6}{8}$ – compound time
c. Syncopation
d. Sequence
e. F minor
f. Tierce de Picardie.

COMMENTS

■ Throughout, the musical substance is the chord progression; the melodic line is formed by the top note of each chord: a classic homophonic texture.

■ Each beat has a long + short subdivision (or 'tum-ti-tum', if you prefer): typical of compound time. There are two beats in each bar.

■ The *sfz* moment in bar 4 does not occur on one of the main beats and thus forms a syncopation.

■ The sequential pattern falls through three bars.

■ The music modulates to the relative minor in the second half.

■ The final chord, in a phrase in F minor, is F major. This is a tierce de Picardie and not a late modulation to F major (which is a distant key from the original tonic of A♭ major).

EXERCISE 18

Here is the music you have just heard:

ANSWERS

a. Fugal
b. Seven times
c. It is played at half speed (rhythmic diminution) and in octaves
d. Major (though it passes through a minor key in the middle)
e. Perfect cadence
f. A suspension – actually three of them!

COMMENTS

■ This piece is contrapuntal: three independent melodic lines. However, there is a regularly recurring melodic theme that is heard at the start and returns in each part at different pitches. This makes the texture fugal. In all, the theme is played seven times.

■ The final entry of the fugue subject is given extra weight by being played in octaves in the bass, and with rhythmic diminution.

Here is the music you have just heard:

ANSWERS

a. Homophonic and antiphonal
b. Circle of 5ths
c. The leading legato phrase is now in the bass register and the answering staccato phrase is now in the treble register.

COMMENTS

The music is clearly chordal in nature, and the texture can therefore be called homophonic. In addition, phrases (and later just individual chords) alternate between treble and bass registers, giving an antiphonal effect to the texture as well.

EXERCISE 20

The instrumentation of the figures is:

1st time	French horn
2nd time	French horn
3rd time	French horn
4th time	Clarinet
5th time	Clarinet
6th time	Cor anglais
7th time	French horn
8th time	Cor anglais
9th time	Flute
10th time	Cor anglais
11th time	Flute

Answers and comments on specimen questions for Unit 1 – Section A: Listening

QUESTION 1

ANSWERS

a. Viola
b. Turn
c. Clarinet
d. Ascending chromatic (1 mark for each word)
e. Major
f. Dominant
g. Melody with accompaniment
h. Perfect
i. $\frac{6}{8}$.

COMMENTS

a. A tricky question – were you tempted to put violin or cello? The viola has a distinctive timbre in between the two – it is well worth being sure you know the difference.
b. It is possible to do this question by elimination, though you should recognise the graceful flurry of notes created by a turn.
c. Hopefully an easy mark here…
d. Did you only write one word? There were two marks…
e. Another easy mark.
f. Could you hear the brighter key at this point? If not did you *think*? This is a Classical-style piece in a major key: second themes in such music are nearly always in the dominant.
g. This is a very good example of melody with accompaniment.
h. A perfect cadence is what you would expect at the end of a musical paragraph in the Classical style.
i. You should have felt the two beats in a bar, but did you spot each beat was subdivided into three to create compound time?

QUESTION 2

ANSWERS

a. Timpani
b. 5th
c.

d. Piccolo and glockenspiel

e. The melody is played in octaves

f. Modal.

COMMENTS

a. The timpani are playing with the bass line.

b. The chords are Dm^9 and Gm^9 with the G a perfect 5th below the D.

c. You should have heard that the first of the missing notes is the same as the last given note in this question; the shape is mostly conjunct and the lead back to the E printed in the question is from a step underneath.

d. If you thought flute, listen again to the piccolo starting the fugue in Britten's *Young Person's Guide to the Orchestra* and compare it with this piece. The glockenspiel – the most common mallet instrument in the orchestra – comprises metal bars and gives the tinkling sparkle clearly audible here.

e. Listen carefully if you missed this: the cellos are playing the melody as well, at a lower octave than the violins.

f. There are no sharpened leading notes here at all, giving a very pastoral, folk quality that is typical of modal music.

QUESTION 3

ANSWERS

a. Violin

b. Arco

c.

d. Diatonic

e. Canonic

f. Perfect

g. The music ends in the same key as it began.

COMMENTS

a. An easy mark, hopefully.

b. Again, should be easy, so long as you know your string playing terminology.

c. The clues you need to spot here are: 1) the first missing note is lower than both of the first two notes that are given; 2) the contour is stepwise and descending; 3) the final note on the downbeat is the same as the next downbeat. It also helps if you realise the first note is the tonic.

d. All being well you have just completed the notation for the first phrase. There are no accidentals; there are more than five pitches used: it is diatonic.

e. Did you spot this? Listen carefully to the piano: it is a bar ahead of the violin, playing the identical melody throughout the excerpt (one octave lower).

f. A conclusive cadence, in which you cannot hear the tonic in the penultimate chord: it therefore has to be perfect.

g. You should be able to hear that the music resumes in the same key as it finishes when you hear subsequent playings. However, around 0:20 it has temporarily moved to the relative minor, so the first of the possible answers cannot be true.

QUESTION 4

ANSWERS

a. Oboe
b. Pizzicato
c. Minor
d. Cellos
e. A rising scale in octaves
f. Flute
g. Circle of 5ths harmony; imperfect cadence; sequence *(1 mark for each)*
h. $\frac{2}{4}$.

COMMENTS

a. No instrument does poignant loneliness as well as a solo oboe; this is a fine example.
b. An easy mark, hopefully.
c. The dark, plaintive mood of this piece is largely due to its minor tonality.
d. The rich tenor register of the cello is a great timbre for an expressive melody such as this one.
e. Hopefully you heard the rising scale, but did you notice that the clarinets are in octaves? Listen carefully…
f. Flutes are usually considered to be high-pitched instruments, but they have a rich, warm tone in their lowest octave, as heard here.
g. Most of the cadences in this passage (at the end of each melodic phrase) are imperfect. (Perfect cadences mark the end of the melody, both in the oboe and cellos.) The melodic sequence and circle of 5ths harmony occur simultaneously, as is often the case.

QUESTION 5

ANSWERS

a. There is a **two**-part texture doubled at **three** different octaves
b. Sequence
c. C major (the dominant)
d. Pedal note
e. Horns and then bassoons
f. 3rd
g. Bar 35 beat 1 or 3
h. Binary.

COMMENTS

a. Central to getting this correct is to remember about transposing instruments. When the title for an instrument includes a note, for example 'in B♭', you must remember that a written C will sound that note. Here we have 'Horns in F' and the first note for the second horn is a *written* C, so that will *sound* F – the F at the octave between the second oboe and the second bassoon. The conclusion is that for this whole phrase these six instruments are providing two lines, each doubled at three octaves. If in doubt: listen.

b. The sequence is straightforward to hear and see, both in the melody and the harmony.

c. The most likely modulation (by far) in the Classical style.

d. The pedal note is played (as reiterated crotchets) by cellos and violas in unison. Given the music has already modulated by this point it is actually a tonic pedal, though only one mark is available so 'pedal' is enough.

e. Again, you have to remember about the transposing horns here... or just listen carefully. The '2 marks' indication shows that two different instruments are required here.

f. Here you need to be sure about reading the alto clef in the viola part. The middle line of the stave is middle C.

g. This kind of a question takes patient and methodical searching. Make sure you give both bar *and* beat number if that is what is required. If you only write the bar number you will not get the mark.

h. Two halves, both repeating and modulating to the dominant at the halfway point make up classic binary form.

QUESTION 6

ANSWERS

a. A turn
b. Ic *or* tonic second inversion
c. V⁷ *or* dominant 7th root position
d. C minor
e. Circle of 5ths
f. A trill
g. An octave
h. Bar 16 *or* 17.

COMMENTS

a. The turns are not shown in the score, but listen carefully...

b. Note there are two marks available: you need to earn both! This is the start of a classic Ic–V⁷–I perfect cadence...

c. ... which continues here.

d. Don't fall into the trap of seeing a key signature and giving the associated major key. Listen: Reicha has gone into the tonic minor.

e. You should be able to hear this, but you can certainly see it in the bass line (played, appropriately enough, by the bassoon).

f. This is easier to hear than the oboe turn: it lasts longer.

g. You have to remember that the clarinet in B♭ is a transposing instrument. Or just use your ears...

h. Again, remember the horn in F is a transposing instrument (sounding a 5th lower: written C sounds F). Then search methodically.

Comments on sample essays for Unit 1 – Section B: Historical Study

Here is an annotated version of the essay on page 39 of the revision guide:

Write an informative account of the introduction in the first movement of this symphony. You should refer to structure, melody, texture, instrumentation, rhythm, harmony and tonality.

Beethoven was born in Bonn in 1770 and was 30 when his first symphony was played for the first time in Vienna. The symphony is written for a large Classical orchestra with a full range of wind instruments as well as trumpets and timpani.[1]

Following the model often used by his teacher Haydn, Beethoven starts his symphony with a slow introduction (marked Adagio molto).[2] This begins with four homophonic[3] bars using the whole orchestra that use a series of dominant 7th chords.[4] The dynamics are typical of Beethoven from the outset, with fp markings on the downbeats. Unusually the strings are playing pizzicato.[5]

A brief linking melody on the violins[6] leads to the middle phrase of the introduction.[7] Here the texture is more complicated. There is a long sustained G[8] in the oboe and clarinet around which the harmony moves.[9] The main melody moves stepwise[10] the violins doubled in octaves. Its rhythm is regular with a crotchet on the 2nd beat of the bar tied to the first of eight semiquavers in the second half of the bar. This creates a sense of forward momentum in the music, despite the slow tempo.[11] The C♯s in bar 7 mean the music has gone to D minor.[12] A second tune of falling 3rds[13] is played by the flutes.[14]

A crescendo in bar 7 moves the music back to f for a more homophonic[15] final phrase to the introduction. Like at the start, there is no real melody here[16] –

---

1   This opening paragraph gives accurate context, but is of limited value in addressing the question.
2   Good context, relevant to question.
3   Successful use of technical vocabulary.
4   This is a rather bland summation of the harmony of these bars. The detail and significance has been glossed over. No mention of the change in harmonic rhythm is made.
5   This is a true observation, but the winds have not been mentioned and there is no suggestion that the candidate can hear the effect of this unusual orchestration.
6   The fact that first and second violins are in octaves could be mentioned.
7   Some awareness of the structure of the introduction is apparent.
8   Technical vocabulary could be used: it is an inverted pedal note; the doubling of this on the clarinet an octave lower is overlooked.
9   The harmony is not analysed, not even the fact that this passage is not primarily root-position chords, unlike bars 1–4.
10 Conjunct would be a better term here.
11 Good description of the detail and effect of the rhythm here.
12 This is absolutely incorrect: the candidate has misinterpreted the significance of the C♯s and cannot have heard the sound of the music in their head when writing this.
13 Triadic would be a good word to use here.
14 Missing detail: the flute line is doubled on first bassoon at a lower octave, enriching the texture.
15 There is also antiphony between strings and winds.
16 The falling four-note shape, which becomes a significant motif, is overlooked.

instead the music is made up of chords such as C major and F major[17] in bar 8 and Ic–V in bar 9.[18] This leads into an interrupted cadence in bar 10.[19] The same chords are repeated in bars 10–12 mainly by the winds.[20] Under their dominant chord in bar 12 the strings play a G major ascending scale before cancelling the F♯ on the way down at the end of the bar so that the music can resolve into C major and the Allegro can begin.[21]

Beginning his symphony with this slow section makes the piece sound important[22] and means there is a big contrast when the tempo changes for the first subject at bar 13.[23] The violin tune here is built out of a three-note motif which is a device Beethoven often used in his melodies. The woodwind chords at bars 17–19 are similar to the chords at the start of the introduction.[24]

Here is an annotated version of the sample essay on pages 41–42 of the revision guide:

Describe the ways in which Beethoven makes use of rhythm in the second movement of this symphony.

Beethoven chooses the tempo 'Andante cantabile con moto' for the second movement of the symphony and writes the movement in ⅜ time.[25] The key is F major.[26] The second violins start the movement with a single melody line.[27] There is a lilting quality to the music because it starts with an upbeat.[28]

The same melody then enters in the violas and cellos, followed by an entry in bar 10 on bassoon and double basses, and then the first violins, flutes and oboes in bar 12. The music is like a fugue at first before settling into a more homophonic texture.[29] The first subject ends with lots of semiquavers in the horns[30] and a lot of sforzandos in the music, which give a jolting effect.[31]

---

17 This is inaccurate: the candidate has wrongly identified the chord. It does have an F in the bass, but is the first inversion of D minor (chord II).
18 Correct harmonic analysis.
19 Correct, though the G♯ in the bass deserves to be mentioned.
20 True; the slower harmonic rhythm could be mentioned.
21 A good description of what happens in this bar. The strings are in octaves.
22 Part of the purpose of this introduction, but its prime function is to establish the tonic key. This has not been mentioned.
23 A rather vague comment.
24 These final two sentences are about the start of the exposition and not really relevant to this question.
25 Factually correct, but only tells the examiner what can be seen in the score. Does not really demonstrate understanding.
26 Not relevant to the question.
27 This is not relevant either.
28 True, but the lilting quality comes as much from the stress on the downbeat that is created by the phrasing and this creates a one-in-a-bar feel. The dotted rhythms in bar 3 – which are of considerable significance – are not mentioned. 'Anacrusis' is a better word to use than 'upbeat'.
29 This paragraph up to this point is not about rhythm and therefore not relevant to the question.
30 This is true up to a point, but the melody again has important dotted rhythms here which are ignored. What is the effect of the horn semiquavers?
31 The candidate has missed the essential fact that some of the *sf* markings do not occur on the downbeat.

The second subject also starts with an upbeat and has a graceful character.[32] After a while there is more energy in the rhythm. In bar 33 there are demisemiquavers[33] and from bar 35 the melody has lots of semiquavers.[34] Then there are lots of dotted rhythms from bar 42.[35] Finally Beethoven uses triplet semiquavers as the exposition comes to an end.[36]

The second half of the movement goes to D♭ major[37] and again has lots of dotted rhythms.[38] Firstly these are played by the strings and then on the timpani as the rest of the orchestra begin to concentrate on simple quavers.[39] Beethoven provides some relaxing contrast rhythmically with two bars when the whole orchestra play dotted crotchets.[40]

Bar 100 is the recapitulation. Here Beethoven returns to his first subject tune, but he also includes lots of semiquavers in the texture to make it sound different from the start of the movement.[41] The second subject, however, is the same as it was before, including the triplet semiquavers.[42] The dotted rhythms return near the end to make a more energetic passage.[43] However, Beethoven ends the movement peacefully with the horns. The rhythm here is reduced to quavers.[44]

---

32 Much more detail can be given here: the unaccompanied downbeats in bars 27 and 29, and the dotted rhythms for the anacruses in bars 28 and 30, for example.

33 These demisemiquavers form a turn figure (in 3rds between first and second violins) and are more about delicacy and ornamentation than energy.

34 The semiquavers (which are in the first violin) are a countermelody: the woodwinds are playing the main second-subject melody. The candidate has clearly looked at the score and not heard the music in their head.

35 More detail and description are possible here. Some dotted rhythms start with a dotted semiquaver rest, whilst others involve ties. What is the effect of these features? The striking rhythms of bars 49–51 with the short–long division of a bar and *sf* markings on the crotchets are not mentioned.

36 An important detail regarding the rhythm of the accompanying texture is missed here: the strings and winds alternate chords in quavers, creating a hemiola effect.

37 Not relevant to the question.

38 A much more telling description could be made of the intensity of the string chords in their dotted rhythms here. Moreover, the wind writing is overlooked here: important things are afoot. Firstly they are picking up on the anacrusis-downbeat pattern that is significant to both first and second subject, then there are second-beat *sf* markings from bar 78.

39 Again, important detail is missing, suggesting that the candidate is not imagining the sound of the music. For bars 81–84 the orchestra maintains the natural stress of the triple time metre, but then pairs of quavers alternate between strings and winds from bar 85, creating more hemiola effects.

40 This seems to be a visual observation rather than an aural one: these dotted crotchet chords carry considerable intensity, being dominant 7th chords.

41 'Different' is not a great choice of word. What is the effect of this countermelody in semiquavers?

42 Much of this recapitulation passage has been glossed over.

43 With a *p* dynamic, does this passage really sound more energetic? The anacrusis–downbeat element in the winds is overlooked.

44 The last reference to the anacrusis–downbeat figure, which is *f* across the orchestra, is not mentioned.

Comments on sample essays for Unit 1 – Section C: Historical Study

Here is an annotated version of the essay on Baroque Choral Music on pages 46–48 of the revision guide.

Choose two contrasting arias from the music you have studied, and write informatively about each.

I am going to write about two arias from Handel's oratorio Messiah, which he wrote in 1741 for a performance in Dublin. The two arias I have chosen are 'The trumpet shall sound' and 'He was despised'.[1]

'The trumpet shall sound' comes in part 3 of the oratorio, and is probably Handel's best-known aria for the bass voice.[2] There is also a very important trumpet part,[3] as suggested to Handel by the text.

There is a long introduction in which the main theme[4] is presented on the trumpet, an immediate response to the text of the previous recitative.[5] There are a few instances of dialogue between the trumpet and the strings.[6] Cadences are decorated by trills in the trumpet, which gives a virtuoso touch.[7] The bass soloist enters in bar 28.[8] His melody is similar to the trumpet tune, and has a rising scale for 'dead shall be raised'. The very long 'A' section has a short interlude in the middle for the trumpet to give the singer a rest.[9] It ends with a dramatic interrupted cadence and a final bar for the singer alone.[10] The trumpet again stars in the postlude.[11]

---

1 Candidates are often tempted to spend time writing about what they are going to write about, but it is just a waste of precious time in the exam room and will not gain any marks. Much better just to start writing about the music. The facts here – year and place – may give a touch of context, but are not very relevant to the question.
2 Again, this sentence has limited benefit.
3 A chance has been missed here to use technical vocabulary: obbligato.
4 Some detail about this trumpet melody would help – the rising arpeggio and dotted rhythms at the start, the conjunct even quavers in the upper register, and so on.
5 Good awareness of the context of the aria in the overall story of the whole piece.
6 More detail about this would be beneficial.
7 True, though a more telling, stylistic point would be to mention that there are hemiolas at the cadences (the aria being in triple time – which is not mentioned here).
8 There is not a lot to be gained from knowing the bar number here: it is a waste of memory. The musical description of the moment is 'the first entry of the bass' and not 'bar 28'; the latter you might muddle up and get wrong, the former is very easy to remember, and very precise.
9 It is true that there is an interlude, but its significance is missed: it articulates the structure of the 'A' section, by occurring when the music has reached a halfway point of cadencing in A major – the dominant. Also, the candidate has referred to 'A' section at this point without first mentioning that the aria is in da capo (or ternary) form.
10 True, although not very clear: the key is not mentioned; neither is the final perfect cadence after the dramatic interrupted cadence.
11 A somewhat informal description. The codetta (not postlude) balances the introduction.

In the middle section, it is the trumpeter who has a rest,[12] as the singer takes over. This middle section makes a contrast, being in B minor[13] and having a more lyrical mood.[14] The whole of the first section is then played again, to finish the aria in a blaze of trumpet sound.

'He was despised' is an alto aria in da capo form,[15] with a strong contrast of mood midway. It begins in a warm E♭ major in a broad Largo tempo. There is a rich string tone in the first bar, but as early as bar 2[16] a falling three-note pattern in thirds, suggestive of falling tears, captures a sense of sorrow. This is reinforced before the introduction is finished by some rich harmony that briefly visits a mournful E♭ minor and has several aching suspensions.[17]

In the 'A' section the soloist's vocal line has many expressive features such as appoggiaturas on 'despised and rejected', several falling scales such as the one on 'sorrows', and the violin melody from the E♭ minor segment of the introduction for the words 'and acquainted with grief'. Perhaps most telling, as the 'A' section comes to a close, is the unaccompanied singing on 'he was despised, rejected' that conveys loneliness, and is punctuated by the tear motif. This is followed by the emotionally charged diminished seventh chord in the orchestra on 'man of sorrow',[18] which is sustained for a bar and a half:[19]

In the middle section, Handel portrays the scourging of Christ on Good Friday[20] through a succession of relentless dotted rhythms in the strings. At the start

---

12   Actually the orchestra is tacet too: the middle section is accompanied only by the continuo instruments.
13   Yes, the middle section starts in B minor, but it modulates to F♯ minor by the end.
14   It would be good to know what musical features makes the middle section more lyrical: an absence of dotted rhythms, long conjunct melismas, sequential patterns, and so on.
15   A clear statement of structure at the start makes further references to structure simple and clear to make in due course.
16   This isn't a feat of bar number memory: it's very easy to remember what happens in the second bar.
17   Lots of good detail about the introduction – instrumentation, melodic shape, harmonic colour – all in an efficient manner.
18   Again, plenty of varied detail, chosen from across the 'A' section. Location has been defined through the relevant words of the text – a much easier way to recall the detail than bar numbers, so long as you can 'hear' the music going through your mind in the exam room. This is why playing and singing it are very valuable ways of revising, not just listening to it. Interact with your music!
19   Quoting the melody and accompaniment for this passage – accurately – is impressive, and supports the analytical comment in an efficient way.
20   Clear awareness of the context of this movement in the story of the oratorio as a whole.

of this section the key has changed to a dark C minor, and it gradually changes to G minor as the music becomes more intense.[21] The harmony through this section is very expressive, with a number of suspensions and a powerful circle of 5ths progression midway through.[22]

The middle section ends dramatically: the orchestra's whipping dotted rhythms suddenly break off, and the alto soloist sings 'from shame and spitting' unaccompanied and in declamatory syllabic style that almost literally spits out the words.[23] A simple but forthright perfect cadence ends the passage before the da capo returns the mood to the aching music of the opening section.[24]

Here is an annotated version of the essay on music theatre on pages 50–51 of the revision guide.

Choose two contrasting solo songs from the music you have studied, and write informatively about each.

I am going to write about 'I could have danced all night' from *My Fair Lady* by Frederick Loewe, and 'Take back your mink' from *Guys and Dolls* by Frank Loesser.[25]

My Fair Lady was a big hit on Broadway in 1956, and is adapted from George Bernard Shaw's play *Pygmalion*. The story is concerned with issues of class: Eliza, a cockney flower-girl, is trained by Professor Higgins to speak like an aristocratic girl, all because of a bet he makes with a friend (Colonel Pickering). The song comes when Eliza, at the end of a long day, finally starts to speak with the proper posh accent.[26] Mrs Pearce tells everyone to go to bed, and the music immediately starts up with an introductory section. The music is energetic and happy, with chirping woodwind chords.[27] The vocal line ('Bed, bed, I couldn't go to bed') is similarly lively, with a fast tempo and short phrases.[28]

The introduction is brief, and soon the main melody is heard. Here the vocal line is rather different: long phrases that include long notes (on 'danced', 'night' and 'more' in the opening phrase, for example) and this makes for a melody that expresses the dreamy mood that Eliza is now in.[29] However, the chirpy and bubbly mood of the

---

21   Accurate knowledge of the structure of the music, **and** awareness of the effect of that structure on the emotional content of the music.

22   Good detail of the harmonic language here. Do you think the candidate learned this, or did they have the music running through their mind when writing the essay?

23   Excellent description of the music and its expressive impact.

24   A good rounding off of the second half of the essay.

25   Candidates are often tempted to spend time writing about what they are going to write about, but it is just a waste of precious time in the exam room and will not gain any marks. Much better just to start writing about the music.

26   Write about the music! This paragraph giving a context for the song can be greatly reduced.

27   These chords could be usefully analysed: they are not just standard triads.

28   The introduction is rather glossed over: there is a structure to it (in two halves) that would bear discussion.

29   A reasonable description of the melody, though the rising arpeggio anacrusis (that throws emphasis onto 'danced') might be mention – after all, it comes twice in the phrase.

introduction is also present in the way the woodwinds accompany the singer with rapid quavers.[30] This makes for a skilful musical portrayal of Eliza's feelings and accounts for the song's popularity. To further intensify the impact of the song, the final phrase ('I only know...') starts with a dramatic hold-back.[31]

The main melody is repeated for a second verse, which includes some counterpoint[32] from the maids trying to help Eliza get to bed.[33] A third verse starts softly, but builds to a big climax, with Eliza finishing on a long sustained top G – an ending sure to inspire applause from the audience.[34]

In 'Take back your mink' there is a slightly longer introduction.[35] Here Adelaide is reminiscing about her relationship with Nathan, and all the gifts he showered upon her. This is captured in the freedom of the rhythm – almost recitative-style[36] – with a sense of natural speech, and pauses between each recollection. The melodic contour twists and turns in conjunct fashion, adding to the conversational flavour.[37] Harmonically, the passage avoids any strong use of the tonic chord, which creates a sense of anticipation (where it is used, a flattened 7th is quickly introduced to move forwards to chord IV). The introduction ends with a prolonged dominant 7th.[38]

The main refrain takes the character of an elegant Viennese waltz – conveying the sophistication of the lyrics (mink, pearls, etc.) and the romanticism of young lovers.[39] The melodic idea is a simple two-bar shape, which is treated to a falling sequence:[40]

---

30 Good awareness of the orchestration in the accompaniment, though the doubling of vocal melody in various octaves on the strings is another important factor that does not get mentioned here.
31 The structure of this refrain is overlooked. It is essentially in 32-bar song form (AABA), but – interestingly – the second phrase is not a direct repeat of the first, staring a tone higher and suggesting sequence. Has the candidate 'heard' the music in the exam room?
32 Good use of technical vocabulary...
33 ...but more detail needed to describe the clever juxtaposition of moods and motifs here.
34 There is little different in the final verse, but mention of the harmony and orchestration at the end could be made perhaps.
35 In writing about this song, the candidate gets to the music straight away.
36 Good vocabulary.
37 A good, efficient description.
38 Excellent awareness of the harmonic writing.
39 Good comment and awareness of context.
40 Quoting the opening eight-bar phrase – accurately – is impressive, and supports the analytical comment in an efficient way.

COMMENTS ON SAMPLE ESSAYS FOR UNIT 1 – SECTION C: HISTORICAL STUDY

The refrain follows the standard AABA song form,[41] and the second line follows a very similar phrase, slightly adjusted at the end. For the third line, however, Loesser changes the metre to $\frac{3}{4}$. This, coupled with a simple vocal line alternating between two notes, shows that the elegance of the waltz was just Adelaide maintaining dignity: now we realise she is in a strop! The waltz metre returns for the final 'A' phrase, and a confident perfect cadence that – finally – conclusively finds the tonic chord.[42]

The scoring of the song is for a dance band: trumpets and saxes to the fore, and some rich bass clarinet on the bass line. There is a very telling short trumpet solo in the opening section at 'one night in his apartment' which calls for the wah-wah mute that gives a suggestive tone.[43]

After Adelaide has sung the refrain, her 'dolls' repeat it in an upbeat $\frac{4}{4}$ version that makes the mood more defiant. A further version for dancing is played as an instrumental.[44]

Here is an annotated version of the essay on British popular music on pages 53–54 of the revision guide.

Choose two songs written in the 1970s, and write in detail about the musical content of each song.

I am going to write about two great songs from the 70s: 'Speak To Me – Breathe' from Pink Floyd's iconic album *The Dark Side of the Moon*, and 'Somebody To Love' by the famous rock band Queen.[45]

Pink Floyd were a London-based band who came to fame in the late 60s with their elaborate light shows. When the line-up changed in 1968, their music changed direction, and became focused on various forms of alienation such as madness and death, which appealed to those growing up in the shadow of Vietnam and the Cold War. *The Dark Side of the Moon* was released in 1973 and is the fifth highest-selling album of all time. 'Speak To Me – Breathe' is the first song on the album.[46]

'Speak To Me' is largely not traditional music but a collage of sound effects starting with a heartbeat, created through a dampened bass drum.[47] Other

---

41 This time the form of the song is clearly stated.
42 Excellent description of the refrain; do you think the candidate learned all this, or did they have the music running through their mind when writing the essay?
43 This paragraph shows the candidate has **listened** to the music attentively – noting significant aspects of the orchestration – and not just relied on the vocal score.
44 This final paragraph is almost superfluous, since the song turns into a chorus and then a dance number, but it succinctly shows that the rest of the song is known.
45 Candidates are often tempted to spend time writing about what they are going to write about, but it is just a waste of precious time in the exam room and will not gain any marks. Much better just to start writing about the music.
46 Unfortunately, interesting though this paragraph may be, this does not address any musical points. This is a music AS exam: write about music!
47 Good detail about timbre and its intended effect.

sounds heard include ticking clocks, manic laughter, a cash register and a helicopter, all sounds which were to reappear in other songs in the album.[48] There are also fragments of conversation about madness layered on top. At the end a reversed piano chord[49] completes the sense of build-up as the track leads immediately on into 'Breathe'.

'Breathe' has a more clearly defined beat at a slow tempo (typical of Pink Floyd) in four-time. The bass drum gives a strong downbeat to the rhythm.[50] There is a more distinct verse structure here: eight lines that come in two halves – a change of chord sequence marking the halfway point.[51] The same music provides an instrumental introduction with guitars and frequent slow pitch-bending.[52] The song links into the next track on the album, 'On The Run'.

As prosperity grew in the 1970s, pop concerts increasingly were held at large stadiums such as Wembley. The song by Queen 'Somebody To Love' is representative of a style that suits such events, a style now called 'stadium rock'.[53] The song is influenced by gospel music, especially of the style sung by Aretha Franklin.[54] Using the latest in 1970s technology, the band members multi-tracked their voices to create the aural illusion of a 100-strong gospel choir.[55]

The introduction to the song is sung with discreet piano backing and has a free approach to rhythm, with frequent pauses, that is typical of gospel music.[56] The voices start on A♭ and fan out in contrary motion in a homophonic choral style.[57]

When the first verse starts the music goes into a strict tempo (a compound four in a bar) and there is a confident, marching quality, heightened by the harmony that concentrates on major chords and keeps moving towards the sharper dominant key.[58] This is achieved by using a B♭ major chord when the song is in A♭ major.[59] Freddie Mercury sings the melody whilst other members of the band provide the backing vocals in a multi-tracked gospel style. The main melody tends to have a

---

48 Shows awareness of context in terms of the album.

49 The reversed piano chord and layering of conversation fragments is good detail, but rather glosses over the significance of the potential for these aspects in 1970s technology.

50 Some good musical details concerning metre and timbre up to this point in this paragraph.

51 There are fewer details here about structure and harmony; information about the chord patterns would be valuable here – in terms of marks.

52 Good use of technical vocabulary here, but the use of synthesisers has been overlooked, which is, surely, a significant factor for 1970s music.

53 There is less biographical flannel here: we start with a significant factor about the way the decade influenced pop music and this song in particular.

54 Good context of style here; it would be helpful to mention an Aretha Franklin song that shows the connection clearly.

55 This sentence shows good awareness of musical idiom and relevant technology of the decade.

56 Good detail here that supports the assertion of the gospel influence.

57 Good use of technical vocabulary regarding the texture here. Do you think the candidate has learned this, or did they have the music running through their mind when writing the essay?

58 Confident analysis of the elements of rhythm and harmony, with good vocabulary and awareness of the resulting emotional affect.

59 Good technical support of the assertion in the previous sentence.

rising contour that allows for some impassioned singing at the top of the male range. Falsetto is also used at times.[60] The 'somebody to love' line provides an infectious melodic hook, and the drumming (by Roger Taylor) makes heavy use of the crash cymbal.[61]

There are two verses, and then a short middle section which provides a balance to the harmony of the verse by visiting the flat side: $D\flat$ major, $G\flat$ major, and $G\flat$ minor. This then passes into an instrumental solo for the lead guitar (played by Brian May), which is based on the chord sequence of the verse. Voices join in at the end and lead into another vocal verse. This, however, breaks off before the refrain, and the line 'need somebody to love' is repeated many times, building from an a cappella start. A final refrain follows.[62]

There is then a coda with several more repetitions of 'find me somebody to love', with rhythmic hand-clapping providing an infectious feature for audience participation: a significant element of stadium rock.[63]

---

60 The candidate has clearly listened carefully to the song and has spotted issues of vocal technique that are audible to the thoughtful listener.

61 Similarly, the candidate has honed in on the playing of the drums and heard this in some detail.

62 This paragraph shows a secure awareness of the structure of the song. It would be possible to present this in table form, which might be something of a time-saver.

63 A neat way to round off this part of the essay.

Glossary

Anacrusis. The note or notes that form an upbeat (or upbeats) to the first downbeat of a phrase.

Antiphony. A technique where two instrumental groups or two choirs alternate in dialogue.

Appoggiatura. An ornamental note that falls on the beat as a dissonance and then resolves by step onto the main note.

Articulation. The manner in which a series of notes are played with regards to their separation or connection – for example, staccato (separated) or legato (connected).

Augmentation. The lengthening of rhythmic values of a previously heard melody (for example in a fugue), or the widening of an interval.

Auxiliary note. A non-harmony note which is a step above (upper auxiliary) or below (lower auxiliary) the harmony note and returns to it.

Binary form. Two-part structure (AB), usually with both sections repeated.

Chord extension. Chords which add additional 3rds to the third and fifth degree of a triad, creating a 7th, 9th, 11th or 13th. You may have encountered some of these in Area of Study 2c.

Chromatic. The use of non-diatonic notes (notes which are not in the current key). Chromatic notes or chromatic passages are often used for expressive purposes.

Circle of 5ths. A series of chords whose roots are each a 5th lower (or a 4th higher) than the previous one. For example, Em–Am–Dm–G–C.

Col legno. A string technique of playing with the wood of the bow.

Compound metre. Time signature in which the beat divides into three: $\frac{6}{8}$, $\frac{9}{8}$, $\frac{12}{8}$.

Con sordino. An instruction to the performer to play with a mute.

Consonant. Intervals or chords which are stable and sound pleasant (for example, unisons, 3rds, 6ths), as opposed to its opposite, dissonant.

Continuo. Short for 'basso continuo', the continuo instruments form the accompaniment in Baroque music. It may include instruments such as the harpsichord (capable of playing full harmony) and a cello or bassoon reinforcing the bass line.

Contrary motion. Movement of two parts in opposite directions to each other.

Counter-melody. An independent melody which complements a more prominent theme.

Da capo aria. Common aria form of Baroque opera and sacred music. ABA shape, with Da Capo instruction at the end of the B section. The singer may add ornamentation during the repeat.

Diatonic. Using notes that belong to the current key.

Diminished 7th. A four-note chord made up of a diminished triad plus a diminished 7th above the root. Diminished 7ths usually function as dominants of the following chord, with the root of the chord omitted in favour of the minor 9th.

Dominant 7th. A four-note chord built on the dominant (5th) note of the scale. It includes the dominant triad plus a minor 7th above the root.

Double stopping. A string technique of playing more than one string at a time. Also triple and quadruple stopping.

False relation. A chromatic contradiction between two notes sounded simultaneously and in different parts. For example a G natural against a G sharp.

Falsetto. This involves the singing of notes above the normal range of the human voice, normally by male singers.

Glissando. A slide between two notes.

Ground bass. Repeating bass, usually four or eight bars in length, with changing music in the other parts. Popular in Baroque music.

Harmonic. Sometimes known as flageolet note, a technique of lightly touching the string (e.g. on a violin) to produce a high, flute-like sound.

Harmonic rhythm. The rate at which harmony changes in a piece.

Hemiola. The articulation of two units of triple time (*strong-weak-weak*, *strong-weak-weak*) as three units of duple time (*strong-weak*, *strong-weak*, *strong-weak*).

Heterophonic. A texture in which different versions of the same melody are heard simultaneously.

Homophonic. A texture in which one part has a melody and the other parts accompany. In contrast to a polyphonic texture, in which each part has independent melodic interest.

Imitation. A contrapuntal device in which a distinct melodic idea in one part is immediately copied by another part, often at a different pitch, while the first part continues with other music. The imitation is not always strict, but the basic melodic and rhythmic outline should be heard.

Leger line. Additional lines used above or beneath the stave to represent notes that fall outside of its range.

Mediant. The third degree of a major or minor scale.

Melisma. A technique in vocal music, where a single syllable is set over a number of notes in the melody. Such a passage may be described as 'melismatic'.

Middle-eight. A passage that may be used in popular music forms, describing a section (usually consisting of eight bars and containing different music) that prepares the return of the main section.

Mode. Seven-note scales that can be created using only the white notes of a piano keyboard. The dorian can be played beginning on D (i.e. D–E–F–G–A–B–C–D), the mixolydian on G, the aeolian on A and the ionian on C. These interval patterns can then be transposed to any other note. For example, dorian beginning on G (or G dorian) would be G–A–B–C–D–E–F–G.

The modes used in 16th-century church music came to interest later composers looking for an alternative to the major-minor tonal system and have been explored in recent times by various classical, jazz and popular musicians.

Modulation. The process of changing key.

Monophonic. A musical texture that uses a single melodic line.

Multi-track recording. A method of recording (normally for popular music) that allows sound sources to be recorded separately and later combined.

Obbligato. Used in Baroque music to denote an instrumental solo part which must be included.

Overdubbing. A recording technique where an additional musical part is recorded to a previously recorded track. This technique is often used by pop musicians to create additional sounds and add more instruments to an existing recording.

Pedal note. A sustained or continuously repeated pitch, often in the bass, that is heard against changing harmonies. A pedal on the fifth degree of the scale (known as the dominant pedal) tends to generate excitement, while a pedal on the key note (known as the tonic pedal) tends to create a feeling of repose.

Phrasing. In performance the execution of longer groups of notes which follow natural patterns of the music. 'Articulation' may be used to refer to phrasing over a shorter group of notes. Phrases may be indicated by the composer but the skill and judgement of the performer is also important in creating a successful performance.

Polyphonic. A texture consisting of two or more equally important melodic lines heard together. In contrast to a homophonic texture, in which one part has the melody and the other parts accompany. The term polyphonic has a similar meaning to contrapuntal, but is more often used for vocal rather than instrumental music.

Portamento. A slide between two notes.

Power chord. A term used in popular music to refer to a chord for guitar that omits the 3rd of the triad. It therefore contains a bare interval of a 5th.

Recitative. A technique in opera and oratorio where the singer conveys the text in a speech-like manner. This is normally used to cover narrative effectively and contrasts with arias which are much more lyrical.

Ritornello. In Baroque music, the repeated tutti section used as a refrain; most often in the first or last movement of a concerto, or in arias or choral works.

Rubato. The alteration of rhythm, particularly in a melodic line, by lengthening and shortening notes but keeping an overall consistent tempo.

Scotch snap. A two-note dotted rhythm which has the shorter note on the beat. Usually an on-beat semiquaver followed by an off-beat dotted quaver. Also known as lombardic rhythm.

Segue. The continuation of one section or movement to another without a break. In popular albums, this refers to one track immediately following its predecessor.

Sequence. Immediate repetition of a melodic or harmonic idea at a different pitch, or a succession of different pitches.

Sonata form. Typical first movement form of the Classical and Romantic periods. In three sections – exposition, development, recapitulation – often based on two groups of melodic material in two contrasting keys (first subject, second subject).

Strophic. A song in which the music is repeated for each verse, for example a hymn.

Sul ponticello. A string technique of playing close to the bridge.

Syncopation. Placing the accents in parts of the bar that are not normally emphasised, such as on weak beats or between beats, rather than in the expected place on strong beats.

Tessitura. A specific part of a singer's or instrument's range. For example a 'high tessitura' indicates a high part of the range.

Through-composed. A stage work (opera or musical) in which the music is not split into seperate numbers. Also a song in which there is different music composed for each verse.

Tierce de Picardie. A major 3rd in the final tonic chord of a passage in a minor mode.

Tritone. An interval that is equivalent to three tones (an augmented 4th or dimished 5th).

Voicing. The arrangement of pitches within a chord to create a particular texture.

Word painting. A technique of setting text in which the sound or movement implied by a word or phrase is imitated by the music (e.g. a falling phrase for 'dying').